Coming Out as Parents

Coming Out as Parents

You and Your Homosexual Child

David K. Switzer

Westminster John Knox Press
Louisville, Kentucky

Scripture quotations from the New Revised Standard Version of the Bible are copyright © 1989 by the Division of Christian Education of the National Council of the Churches of Christ in the U.S.A. and are used by permission.

Book design by Jennifer K. Cox
Cover design by Alec Bartsch

First edition

Published by Westminster John Knox Press
Louisville, Kentucky

This book is printed on acid-free paper that meets the American National Standards Institute Z39.48 standard. ∞

PRINTED IN THE UNITED STATES OF AMERICA

96 97 98 99 00 01 02 03 04 05 — 10 9 8 7 6 5 4 3 2 1

Library of Congress Cataloging-in-Publication Data

Switzer, David K., date.
    Coming out as parents : you and your homosexual child / David K. Switzer
        p.   cm.
    Rev. ed. of : Parents of the homosexual. Philadelphia : Westminster Press,
1980.
    Includes bibliographical references.
    ISBN 0-664-25636-8 (alk. paper)
    1. Parents of gays. 2. Gays—Family relationships. 3. Parent and child. 4. Homosexuality—Religious aspects—Christianity. 5. Parenting—Religious aspects—Christianity. I. Switzer, David K., Parents of the homosexual. II. Title.
    HQ76.3.U5S94   1996
    306.874—dc20   96-16036

Contents

Preface

Parents of the Homosexual appeared in 1980, the result of a request to me from Wayne Oates, Ph.D., a series editor for The Westminster Press, to write a book that would be helpful to parents who are in some way related to the church and who have discovered that a child of theirs is gay or lesbian.

After its publication I received quite a variety of letters and phone calls, as well as a number of comments from gays here in the Dallas area. Most of the letters were from appreciative people: gays who had given the book to their parents who in turn had found help from it; a denominational fellowship of gays and lesbians who were buying a number of copies for distribution; an agency in England engaged in helping services to gays and lesbians and their parents and who could not find a place to purchase the book in that country. (I sent them several copies without charge.)

Within the last few years I have had an increasing awareness of the need for a revision of the book. Just a year or so after its appearance, one gay man expressed to me appreciation for much that was in it. But he was very unhappy about one section and said that he wished it had not been in the book. I agreed with him. It needed to be deleted.

In the years after that, and especially since 1978–79 when the material was being written, so much has taken place. Although the book continues to be sold and read, I have become more and more uneasy about some of the material contained in it and especially about what was *not* in it.

First, none of us knew anything at all about AIDS at that time. Of course, we realize now that the disease is not limited to homosexual males. In fact, in many sections of the country the occurrence of

AIDS is decreasing in that population. Yet gay men are the ones who are dying with increasing frequency at this time.

Second, physiological/genetic research has increased in amount and quality as scientists have attempted to discover clues that explain why some persons are homosexual when the majority of people are heterosexual. Certain findings over the last few years have led me to modify my earlier position, and I believe parents and other concerned persons need to know about these findings.

Third, the last few years have also seen an increasing number of gay and lesbian persons being more open about their sexual orientation. Older and younger adults and even teenagers are telling at least a few friends and family members in greater numbers than they did fifteen years ago. More gay couples and lesbian couples are living together in committed, loving relationships, and many of them are doing so openly. We are witnessing a changed social scene and much greater awareness of the number of gays and lesbians among us.

Fourth, there is an increased public focus on the variety of issues surrounding homosexuality that our society is attempting to deal with: the role of gays and lesbians in business, industry, and the military, as well as the basic civil rights of gays, lesbians, and others.

Fifth, the church is dealing more openly with the biblical, ethical, and practical issues in regard to homosexuality, urged on by increased understanding, compassion, fairness, and, to be honest, insistent pressure. Condemnation of homosexuality and gays and lesbians by some clergy and other representatives of the church is more open and more impassioned. Among the practical issues are ministry to gays and lesbians, their role in the local congregation, ordination to the ministry of a particular church or denomination, and others.

All this is naturally having an influence on families with gay or lesbian members, and these changes have combined to create a genuine urgency to reissue this book. The basic thesis remains the same as the earlier one, and much of the material in the book is identical to that of the earlier edition. But the deletions, changes, and additions are significant.

I want to express my appreciation to Timothy Staveteig, Acquisitions Editor for Westminster John Knox Press, for his encouragement of the revision and his support along the way. My work was made much easier and more pleasant by the efficiency and wonderful attitude of Ann Ralston, a staff member of Perkins School of Theology, who produced the copy that was sent to the publisher.

Introduction

This book is primarily for parents who suspect or have just recently discovered that their son or daughter is gay, lesbian, or bisexual, and it is particularly for those parents whose Christian faith and participation in the church has some meaning. It is my sincere desire that what is said here will be helpful to you in what for many families is a disturbing and even stressful situation.

If you have gotten hold of this book and read to this point, however, but do not have any religious affiliation or any particular religious concerns, *don't stop yet.* In the first place, I don't believe that religion alone makes an essential difference in the emotional reaction to the discovery that one's son or daughter is or may be homosexual. Second, I don't believe that the explicit references to the resources of faith and the biblical material will stand in the way of your receiving some important insights and perhaps emotional support. (After all, you can always just skip chapter 9.)

Other family members are not meant to be excluded by this initial statement. Brothers, sisters, grandparents, and others must deal with their reactions as well. (Spouses who discover that a mate is gay or lesbian or children who discover this about a parent may also profit from reading this book, but to address the unique differences in their situations would carry the discussion away from the narrower focus intended and make this a longer and more complex book.)

Of course, not everything described in the following pages will necessarily coincide exactly with your reactions or needs. That can't be, because people and situations differ so radically, even where there is a core experience that is the same or at least somewhat similar. The terrain over which I shall walk with you is still not completely explored. It may seem strange, confusing, and sometimes unpleasant. The book is yet to be written about which even a majority of people can say, This is it, definitively. Obvious reasons exist for divergence on the issues we will be discussing here.

First, people's experiences differ. Gays and lesbians experience themselves differently from one another, and events differ. Their parents differ from one another emotionally and in their relationships with their children and in their knowledge of homosexuality and the gay life.

Second—perhaps this should have been listed first because of its tremendous influence—this is obviously a highly charged subject emotionally. It certainly is for most parents and other family members. Part of the reason is that when the topic of homosexuality is discussed, it frequently involves some combination of ignorance, prejudice, fear, and anxiety on the part of a large number of people in this and many other countries; most of these people are also members of families. It is certainly not surprising, then, that when parents discover *their own* son or daughter is homosexual these reactions are intensified. Even for fairly well-informed people who are committed to the basic rights of all persons, who are liberal in outlook, who are basically compassionate and understanding, when it is *their own* son or daughter, emotionally somehow it all becomes different, at least for a while.

Third, the subject is also highly charged emotionally for gay persons themselves. It is *their* life. *They* have frequently had problems adjusting to *themselves* as they are. It often places an emotional barrier between them and their parents, whether the parents know or don't know. *They* have been the butt of jokes and had to keep their mouths shut. *They* have been the target of discrimination, prejudice, often direct verbal abuse, and sometimes physical attack. It is certainly an emotional area for them.

Finally, to be quite candid, even professional researchers and helping persons have yet to reach absolute consensus on what "causes" homosexuality. Legal definitions and pronouncements are mixed and constantly changing. The military is still in a quandary about legal rights and obligations. Christians and Jews and the nonreligious as well have not determined what *the* biblical position is on it. Researchers have formed varying theories based on differing and incomplete data that have been accumulated by different procedures and drawn from different populations of homosexual persons. They make different interpretations of their observations, and therefore on the basis of their present positions, they support different courses of action. Undoubtedly, some just plain have their own personal opinions and feelings. Such differences among conscientious, honest, and competent people should give us all cause to temper our remarks with some degree of tentativeness. One researcher, regarding the origin of homosexuality, may say, "This is definitely what I have discovered." And it is. But that doesn't necessarily mean that a single discovery covers all cases. One homosexual person may say, "I know *this* is the reason I'm gay, and this is the way my life is for me." And that may be so, but others may have still different experiences. One parent may say, "This is what it's like in *our* family," but this observation doesn't describe all families. One biblical scholar says a word means one thing and another scholar says it means something else, or they come to different conclusions using what seems to be the same information. Overall, it is a complex and even confusing picture. However, accurate information *is* available, and it can be pieced together to form clearer pictures than some that perhaps we have accepted up until this time. The task of putting differing material together is what this book sets out to do.

But why? I am writing this book mainly out of a deep concern for parents and their sons and daughters and for other family members who are going through this difficult and agonizing time within themselves and with one another. I draw mainly on my experiences with young people and adults who are homosexual, with their parents, with other family members, and with persons who discover that their spouse is gay or lesbian. I trust that what you learn here will help you better understand yourselves and your son or daughter or brother or sister or spouse, and that you will find guidance and support in what is for many parents and spouses in this situation a time of extreme stress, conflict, and self-examination. I hope the book will play some role in your movement toward genuine reconciliation and mutual love and respect in your family. This is its ultimate goal.

I also know that we may have differing interpretations of portions of the Bible and may come to different conclusions on some of the key issues. While I naturally think I have good reasons for interpreting scripture as I do (which you will read in chapter 9), I have learned that equally sincere Christians and conscientious persons do not always share the same beliefs. While all of us are basically united in faith, we look at things from a variety of perspectives and thus have differing beliefs. It is in the sharing of these that we learn and grow and are strengthened in our life and faith.

Regardless of what you might now believe about the various issues, you need to realize that your positions on them must not be allowed to interfere with your dealing effectively with the confusion and emotional distress that you as parents or as other family members may be undergoing, with the stress that is usually placed on the relationship between yourselves, and with your need to understand and have a good relationship with one another. I am convinced that regardless of a person's position on different issues, the essential tasks that I outline in this book are *necessary* to accomplish and *can* be accomplished.

Having made a concerted effort to look at many books on homosexuality, yet knowing well that there are many I have not yet seen, I have found only four that were specifically written for parents (see the Additional Resources section at the back of this book). Each of these books has genuine value. Whereas three of them take into consideration the reader's religious background and participation and show a respectful attitude toward what is meaningful to the reader, none deals explicitly with religious issues in any detail. One of them (Fairchild) does have a good chapter on this topic, but the book is not directed *primarily* toward people related to the church.

Even though this book is particularly for parents, and to some extent for other family members (and much of the language will indicate that), I certainly hope that gay and lesbian persons will read it to provide themselves with the groundwork for a better understanding of what their parents may be going through now or might go through at whatever time that they learn about their children's sexual orientation. Unexpected reactions of parents (such as a mild initial reaction but then later a great deal of hurt and anger), behavior that is extreme (*great* anger, threats, blame), or behavior that is even more undesirable than those just mentioned (abject self-blame, uncontrollable weeping, depression), may all be understood as normal, given the parents' situation and perspective, and as transient, especially if both the gay or lesbian person and his or her parents are dedicated to "hanging in there" for a time as they continue to communicate with one another.

Who am I to dare to write a book like this? Especially when a book addresses a situation as problematic as homosexuality in the family, it may be important to many readers to know what qualifies me to discuss it, to know something of my experience and perspective. I am heterosexual (in case you were wondering) and very happily married. I am a retired minister who has served local churches, been a college chaplain, was a counselor for several years to students and their families at a theological seminary, then was a full-time teacher of pastoral care and counseling at that school and a part-time psychiatric hospital chaplain at the same time. I have known personally homosexual persons in all these settings and have sometimes known their parents. I have talked with these young persons about their relationships with their parents and vice versa. In addition, a number of psychologists and psychiatrists have referred parents to me for counseling that focused on their reactions to and relationships with a child who is gay or lesbian. I have learned a great deal from all these people. I am also a parent of two grown, married children and know something of what it is to love them deeply: to have and let go, to experience conflict, to suffer with them. I also have a young daughter whose unknown future stretches ahead for many years.

Coming as they do out of my experience, the events and conversations I refer to here are those of real persons in anguish and conflict, struggling to understand, trying to make sense out of their situation, attempting to reach a point of resolution. Much of what is reported here is done so with the full knowledge and permission of those involved, but in all instances, a variety of factors such as location, sex, and other kinds of identifying details in these situations have been rendered anonymous or changed or made into a composite picture.

1   *Oh, No!*

He came into the kitchen while his father and I were having a cup of coffee. He looked so serious that we stopped our conversation and I asked him if anything was wrong. He didn't answer, just got a cup of coffee for himself, and sat down at the table with us. He took a long time to stir in the sugar and cream and didn't look at me even once. Finally he said, "I want to tell you something, and it's the hardest thing I've ever had to do." I felt my stomach begin to knot up and noticed that my son's face seemed drawn and pale. I glanced at my husband and he was just staring grimly down into his cup. We all seemed frozen in place for a minute, and then our son blurted out, "I'm gay!" I couldn't believe it. I felt dizzy and sick, and my child seemed an absolute stranger. I thought, Oh no! Not my son! Not that bright, dear little child that I had read to, tucked into bed, who had been his grandparents' favorite and the teachers' pet. There had to be some ghastly mistake.

"Oh, no!"

We all have said these words. They are the very natural, immediate, spontaneous response of any human being to some event or to the report of some event or to some other information that is first experienced as being unbelievable or emotionally intolerable to us.

"Did you hear that Joe had a heart attack?"

Or ". . . that Mary's son was killed in an automobile accident?"

Or ". . . that Sue is an alcoholic?"

Or "I hate to break this news to you, but the tests show that you have cancer."

Or— Add your own experience: your family, your friends.

"Oh, no!" We don't even think about the words. They force

themselves out instantaneously as the genuine expression of our denial that this is so, of our desire that it *not* be so.

"Mom, Dad, I have something to tell you. I'm gay."

"Oh, no!"

The words of the mother in the incident just described are fairly typical. "You *can't* be. Why, you are *our* child. You must be wrong. This must be a sick joke. Don't tell me. Don't think about it."

At some level, these words represent the internal response that parents make to a thought and a group of feelings that they feel they cannot bear. Everything in them combines to reject it. Few events are more painful to parents than getting the news that their son or daughter either has been forced into in some way or has chosen a course in life that is counter to a value system that they, the parents, hold dear and/or counter to the expectations, whether conscious or unconscious, spoken or unspoken, that all we parents have for our children.

This is especially true when sons or daughters announce to their parents that they are gay or lesbian, or when parents get this word from someone else. Even for parents who have suspected for a period of time that this might be the case, and many do, it still comes as a shock. For some parents, homosexuality is seen to be desperately, desperately wrong morally. It is radically out of kilter with the way things are supposed to be; it is "unnatural," "against nature," "sick." Even among parents who view themselves as enlightened, who have an intellectual understanding of what homosexuality is that allows them to be tolerant if not accepting of gays and lesbians, when it is *their* child it is different. Something deeply buried emotionally rises to the surface and tries to reject this reality.

Shock and denial have been clearly identified and their role in our lives investigated in connection with a number of other major life crises. Among them are two very common ones. Dr. Elisabeth Kübler-Ross, in her book *On Death and Dying,* reports the results of her interviews with more than two hundred terminally ill patients. She states that the initial reaction to the discovery of their illness for nearly all of them was denial: "No, not me; it cannot be true."[1] They experience a combination of both intellectual rejection of the fact and emotional numbness, the experience of "no feeling at all." This reaction is as natural a response by the person's mind and emotions to an overwhelmingly painful reality as that of the body's shock reaction to severe physical trauma. It is a buffer, a temporary protection against the pain, allowing the person some time to mobilize other defenses and resources to help deal with the distress. It serves the purpose of allowing the impact of reality to filter through into the conscious mind in smaller amounts. Slowly, then, by bits and pieces, the whole truth may be assimilated, and in varying degrees, accepted.

The same initial experience is observed in dealing with grief, and all authorities list shock, numbness, and denial as typical of the first stage. Dr. C. Murray Parkes, a British research psychiatrist, speaks of the "blunting" of the emotions that comes on very quickly after the death of a person with whom we have close emotional ties.[2] This emotional blunting, Parkes has discovered, lasts from a few hours to a few days, although sometimes it may last even longer. He reports an interview with one woman who found her husband's body on the stairs. The first stab of pain expressed itself with loud and long wails. But within a few minutes she began to feel numb all over. "I felt numb and solid for a week. It's a blessing." She realized that the numbness covered the pain and enabled her to cope with her children during that time, to make arrangements for the funeral, and to deal with the details of the gathering family. Yet for many persons, along with the numbness comes an underlying sense of impending disaster.

Numerous parents have reported that their reaction to the knowledge that their child is homosexual was similar to what they would feel on losing the child. It was to them as if the child had died. Some even said that it felt worse than a death to them because of their many complicated feelings, because they shared the larger society's abhorrence of the very thought of homosexual feelings and behavior. The denial and shock that is reported as being part of the first stage of one's knowledge of a terminal illness and of grief is also usually part of the first stage of the reaction to hearing about a child's or other family member's homosexuality. "Oh no! It can't be true. Not *our* child—Not *my* spouse." During the first hours and days following such a discovery, some parents report a sense of unreality about it all, just as a person in grief feels. Parents will catch themselves looking out of the corner of the eye at the son or daughter; there is a shudder, and then comes the unreal feeling that it is all a terrible dream. It *cannot* be so. The parents expect any minute to hear the words, "It's all been a mistake." But for most, these words do not come.

We parents have typically invested so much of ourselves in our children that much of the pain and disorder of their experience or of their misbehavior produces pain in us also. This is natural. Even beyond this, though, there are some parents whose own sense of identity has been so shaky as individuals that they have now begun to find their identity *only* as parents of their children or of a particular child. They have sought to live out their own lives through the lives of their children. For such parents, any disappointment or disillusionment with their children is a particularly distressing blow to them. It is a severe threat to the meaning of their own lives.

Accompanying our investments in our children are our expectations of them. Most of us would prefer to say that we really have none. We only want them to be healthy and happy. But also for most of us, whether we admit it or not, we rather naturally have our own images of what our children's happiness looks like. We may not explicitly tell them that they must finish high school or go to college, but it simply never occurs to us that they won't. We may not put external pressure on them to take over the family business or follow a parent into his or her job. In fact, we may well criticize other parents for doing precisely this. But if the child is *too* different (the boy who wants to be an artist or a dancer or an interior designer, or the girl who wants to be an airline pilot or a construction worker), we discover that something emotional in us resists the child's desire, and we offer very logical reasons to try to get across to this child why he or she should not do this.

Among the usually unspoken expectations we have is that our children will be heterosexual, and will marry and have children. This is usually unspoken (at least until the child reaches about age 22 to 24, or older, depending upon our own particular subculture and family tradition), because it never even occurs to most of us to question whether this is what is going to happen. It is a very deeply ingrained notion within us that heterosexuality, marriage, and children is the way life is and always will be. Every aspect of this wishful expectation is destroyed by the revelation, however it comes to parents, that their son or daughter is gay or lesbian.

Most teenagers and young adults who suspect or think or know that they are homosexual are extremely reluctant to tell their parents directly about it. Some are ashamed. They themselves may be confused and not understand it, and often, at least for a while, they have the same feelings about *themselves* that they expect other persons would have if they knew. Some are terrified as they imagine their parents' reactions. Some withhold because they are angry with their parents. Some don't tell because they genuinely don't want to hurt other family members. But the pressures created by maintaining a facade over the years begin to take their toll, and sooner or later the teenager or young adult realizes that this reality may need to be shared with the rest of the family. It is an awful moment, as much so for the homosexual person as for the parents.

Often the young persons or young adults will reveal the information about their homosexuality in a serial fashion over a period of time. They will drop different clues, hoping that someone else will initiate a conversation that will lead ultimately to the needed revelation. Also often enough, they will test the impact of the information first on a brother or a sister who has been a trusted friend with the hope that this person's reaction will encourage them to move on to a parent or to both parents. Or they may hope that the brother or the sister will tell their parents for them. If their relationship with their brother or sister has been good, if there have been many shared experiences, it is likely that the first response will not entail so much shock, because there is usually not the same kind or intensity of emotional investment between siblings as there is between parents and their children. The revelation to a brother or sister can serve as a signal concerning parental "readiness." In addition, when the time comes to inform the parents, a brother or a sister can be prepared to be a support to the lesbian or gay sibling and serve as a buffer between her or him and their parents.

A young man shares his experiences:

> I hinted around for weeks to my sister and finally just took my friend, who was also my lover, over to her house for dinner. I introduced him to her and she said: "My brother has told me so much about you. I almost feel like I'm meeting his fiancée." Then she really blushed and we all started laughing like crazy. I remember that I also felt like crying. When we finally calmed down, I said, "You knew all along, didn't you?" She said, "You mean that you and Jim are more than roommates? Yeah, I figured you guys were gay a long time ago, and you know what? It's okay with me." Then I did cry some and hugged her and told her I sure wished she had told me a long time ago. It was like a lot of tension went out of my body. Now the big job is my mom and dad.

In this case the young man went on to tell his parents. Even though they had suspected for some time that he was homosexual, the clear announcement of it was still a shock. The mother cried and the father was grim. It was a difficult situation, but the sense of the sister's support had helped him do what was important to him.

A young woman tells of a quite different initial reaction:

I told my sister I was in love with a woman, and she said that I couldn't be because I was married and had a kid. I told her I was getting a divorce and moving in with my lover and that we were going to raise my daughter. She told me that I was crazy and she didn't want to hear any more and that I sure hadn't better tell my folks because it would kill my father. I felt bad a long time after that because my sister and I had been really close and never did have any secrets from each other. But that's turned out okay. We're cool with each other now.

After beginning to work things out with her sister, she went on to tell her mother. The mother, like the sister, was stunned and hurt. But in the midst of her pain, she responded, "Your father must never know. It would just kill him." Poor father, so vulnerable, protected from the real world by all the women in his life.

"But we are Christians. We've been active in the church. Our son has grown up in the church. He knows what the Bible says about homosexuality." The outcry of How could this possibly happen to us? is natural and understandable as a cry of anguish. The Bible has many comparable spontaneous outbursts of pain and confusion: "If we're God's chosen people, why are we allowed to suffer, to be defeated?" and so forth.

But the Bible itself also makes it clear that no protection is promised against the many possible threats that are inherent in life: sickness, pain, death, distress of many kinds. To be sure, it contains references to God as a rock, a shield and a buckler, a very present help in trouble; many other expressions as well reinforce the experience that God is a present strength and support, and that, no matter what the immediate circumstances, God is still with us and will also be with us in the future. But the same realities of life are the common experience of *all* humanity. "God sends rain on the just and on the unjust."

Some children who grow up in Sunday school and church, in Christian homes, somewhere along the line realize that they have sexual feelings for a person of their own sex. If they have parents who are active members of the church, these parents then experience shock, followed by the anguish and mental and emotional confusion that overcomes them upon the discovery that their child is lesbian or gay.

The purpose of this book is to try to help you if you suspect or have learned for certain that your child (or some other family member) is gay or lesbian. The book attempts to assist you in dealing with what is going on in your situation by discussing some of the major questions and thoughts and feelings that others have experienced in similar circumstances: the denial, the grief, the blaming of others and oneself, the anger, the shame, the confusion. If you have any or all of these feelings, you are normal. More often than not, they are to be expected.

I also hope to give you in brief summary the best information I have regarding what homosexuality is, what the meaning of the Bible may be to you and your family in this situation, how your own thoughts and feelings may begin to change, and how healing and reconciliation may begin to take place in the family.

Reconciliation can come. It does not *always*, but it may: if the son or daughter is candid and kindness is mutual; if he or she can understand and be patient with the rather understandable first "Oh, no," the denial, and the other negative reactions that most parents have; if the gay or lesbian person does not take as the final word any of the many hurtful things parents may say as they begin to deal with their own new and strong feelings and confusion; if parents can be more understanding of their own initial reactions so they may then focus their efforts on trying to understand their child through many long conversations; if the parents can give themselves and their children the time to allow the love between them that is still really there to rise to the surface and become the most influential of their variety of feelings.

This chapter opened with a mother's story of her young son who told his parents he was gay. Their initial reaction was shock and denial. "Oh, no!" It was an intolerable thought, and the feelings were painful. For a while the parents simply put the information away. They refused to talk about it with each other. But time went on, and with its passing came understanding and healing. This process was aided by the willingness and courage of parents and son alike to accept the possibility that there could be a renewed relationship beyond the pain and disagreement. In this family the son is now accepted as he is. His parents are proud of his work in his chosen profession, and they thoroughly enjoy his company. This is a goal well worth working toward.

2   We've Lost Our Child

When my son finally was able to get across to me that he was gay, it was like being told that he was dead. Suddenly the person sitting across from me wasn't my son anymore. I felt as if I were talking with a stranger.

This father was describing the powerful experience he had when in the midst of talking with his son, the information that this young man in his late twenties was homosexual suddenly came through to him and transformed the scene. A stranger was telling this man that his son had died. The stranger looked like his son. The voice was the same. But the son as the father had known him was dead.

The father discovered that he could not look his son directly in the eyes; he couldn't touch him; he couldn't embrace him. He felt dead inside himself. He felt empty. It was only after many months of tension and pain, and after a minister talked with them both and helped them express their confusion, disappointment, anger, and love, and their desire to work for a better relationship, that the father was able to put his arms around his son and hold him.

Another young man was telling of the reaction of his father to this unwelcome news:

They lived in different parts of the country, so the son wrote his parents that he was gay and was "coming out," that is, beginning to live openly as who he was sexually. Then when they talked next on the phone, the father exclaimed in a rage, "It's a good thing you're not around here. I'd kill you." After a pause in the account, I said to the young man: "I imagine you can probably understand your father's tremendous anger toward you. After all, you killed his son." The young man responded with genuine realization of what that statement meant: "Yeah! Yeah, I guess I did."

In chapter 1, I spoke of the initial sense of shock and the natural tendency to deny the reality of what we are being told. I compared this reaction with that which people have in crises in which they experience reality as being so painful or angering as to be utterly intolerable. It is, as mentioned, also typical of the first stage in grief.

It is very common for parents initially to experience the fact of their son's or daughter's homosexuality as if that person had died. Rationally, everyone can tell that it is not *objectively* a loss. The person is right there: alive, talking, usually wanting to be the child of his or her parents. But at another level, it is inevitable that many parents, in varying degrees, of course, experience the revelation as a death: the loss of the valued person whom they thought and felt they had, the loss of a dream, of an illusion. A number of parents have used precisely that language with me.

We parents invest so much in our children. At first they are totally, absolutely dependent upon us for physical, emotional, and spiritual sustenance. They are dependent on us to learn the behavior that will help them survive, grow, enjoy relationships, become competent. We can see over the years the ways in which they learn what we consciously and unconsciously teach them. We love them, and we are quite aware of their responsiveness to us, even when some of that responsiveness is expressed as anger when they are frustrated. We invest *ourselves* in them. It is difficult for us to think of our future without a continuing relationship with them, and their future involves us. In a very real sense, our own being is tied up with theirs and theirs with ours. We experience them as extensions of ourselves. They literally become a part of us.

All this is unavoidable, given the totally helpless state of the newborn. Yet we are well aware that the task of good parenting is to assist our children through the years to become more and more their own persons, less dependent upon us, more autonomous. We try to live with them and teach them so they develop a value system that is genuinely their own, values that operate within their lives apart from us. Many times, for both children and parents, this process of their becoming less dependent and more autonomous is a wrenching, agonizing one—the pulling apart hurts. The growing separateness may at times feel like rejection or alienation. Considering the mutual investments in one another, the identifications with one another, we begin to understand that when a child or a parent dies, we experience not only a loss of someone "out there" but also a loss of part of ourselves. *We* feel dead or empty. We experience the terrible pain of a vital part of our own selves being torn out of our own "insides."

But death, as we all know, is not the only form of loss. There are many ways in which parents have felt the loss of a child from something other than physical death. For many parents, the discovery that their son or daughter is homosexual is experienced as a loss of the *child* because it *is* a loss of so many elements that have until that moment made up the relationship between the parent and the child: our *interpretation* of who our child is, which, with most parents, has never included even the possibility that the child might be anything but heterosexual; the dreams and expectations of who they would become (married, "respectable" members of the community and the church, having children of their own, which obviously includes our dreams about who *we* will become, namely, grandparents to their children). We have assumed they would continue pretty much the lifestyle that our family has had, accept our value system, always be a part of "our group" (and by implication not be a part of a group of which "we" don't approve). To the extent that we have actually seen parts of ourselves in our children as they have grown up, it now feels as if these parts are being rejected by them, as if we are no longer their parents and they no longer our children.

Silverstein recounts in detail the story of Amy Peterson after her daughter told her that she was gay. She had different reactions during the day: first, very little at all, but later the feeling of being sick.

> That night Amy Peterson had a nightmare. She was standing in front of a pair of large doors, with a big keyhole in them. A man came over with the keys and opened the doors. He pushed them wide apart. They opened upon a big gymnasium, brightly illuminated with floodlights. In the center of the gym was a row of long tables, and on each table there were four small black caskets. The top of each casket was open, and they all contained dead infants. Around the tables were men and women dressed in black. They were

parents mourning for their children, the women beating their breasts. She noticed one woman in particular who was wailing over her dead child. Amy walked toward the woman. She stood by the table and saw that the wailing woman was herself, and the dead infant was Susan. Amy awoke, shaking, and realized that she was coming to think of her daughter as dead.[1]

I don't want to overstate this point, because such a drastic reaction does not occur with all parents to this degree. However, I have observed that most parents, when they first discover their son or daughter is homosexual, display some aspects of this feeling that they have lost their child. In this sense, parents experience grief, with all its complexities. If this is a valid comparison, then it means that the parents' response to this new knowledge is not going to be satisfactorily dealt with in just a few hours or days, nor is it just going to go away by itself with the passing of time. Grief is a process with several identifiable stages. It takes some amount of time to go through each one. A number of things are necessary or important to assist persons in going through these stages constructively. To understand the sense of loss of or estrangement from one's child as being like grief can be very helpful to a parent in a number of ways.

1. You are going through a process that is peculiar not just to you but one that is shared by most persons at one time or another.

2. Your first reactions will probably not persist with the same intensity you feel now. They will tend to diminish.

3. The intensity of feelings, the conflicts, the confusion, and the behavior that results are not abnormal, unless the behaviors become unusually extreme or unless the feelings and behavior persist unabated after six to eight months to a year.

4. It will probably take quite some time for you to adjust to your feelings and thoughts about yourselves and your child, so you need to be tolerant of yourselves and explain to your child his or her need to be tolerant of you during the process.

5. You need to be aware of, accept, and talk frequently about

your feelings and confusion, even if this becomes repetitive.

6. To share all this openly within the family is very important. You need to let every other family member know where you are with your thoughts and feelings at any given time.

7. The support of understanding and trusted persons outside the family (friends, minister, other counselor) can be helpful in diminishing the intensity of your feelings.

8. As in death, this event is a challenge to faith. Some people become angry with God and question God; some reject God. But many find that a deep trust in the compassionate, forgiving, sustaining God is in fact strengthening and hope-full.

My purpose here is to assist you to understand more clearly what is going on within you, what you might expect to experience, and therefore to help you feel somewhat better about yourself and to deal more constructively with yourself as a person, with your spouse, and with your child. In order to accomplish these goals, let us take a more detailed look at the stages of grief.[2]

We have already stated that the first stage is *shock and denial.* Certainly we all can understand this, and we all have experienced shock in other instances. Denial takes numerous forms, but none is so clear as what may stand as a classic response on the part of one mother when her daughter told her she was gay. "Oh no you're not," the mother answered immediately, and she went right on with the conversation on an entirely different subject, as if the daughter had said nothing more startling than, "It's going to rain today." This daughter was twenty-five years old at the time.

One young man had the following impression of his parents' reaction when he first told them. "It was as if they were beyond emotion. It was like a scene in which they'd just received a message that their son was dead, and they seemed to be treating me simply like the man who delivered the death message. Mother began to weep. They expressed disappointment, but after a while they just weren't able to talk any longer."

Parents in this time of first discovery often report a sense of unreality, as if this scene were just a dream. Or they themselves feel unreal, or the whole world about them feels unreal. This is characteristic of shock and is not to be feared. It is a normal reaction.

Of course, other feelings may be a part of the initial reaction to the extent that shock and denial are not complete, as they often are not. Among responses that persons report are feeling sick at their stomachs or feeling sick all over, a sense of impending disaster, as if one's world is crumbling, a stabbing pain, anguish, trembling, feeling faint, or perhaps great anger. The first stage may last only a few hours or days, but it is often longer if parents are able to maintain their denial. It is certainly natural to want to maintain the belief that what they have heard is not so.

The second stage of grief comes with the diminishing of shock and as the reality of the son's or daughter's life as it has now been described to us is reinforced in a number of ways. Parkes calls this stage *yearning*. It includes a variety of strong and often conflicting feelings and those behaviors which seek, in the case of death, to keep the deceased alive, to find the person, or in some instances to join the person where he or she is. In the awareness of your child's homosexuality, just as you would feel at his or her death, there will be pain, anguish, anger, guilt, and confusion. You will feel dead or empty inside and sad. You may also experience revulsion, nausea, weeping, sleeplessness, loss of appetite, and difficulty in acting in your customary natural and spontaneous ways with your son or daughter. For instance, you may find that you withdraw the physical expressions of your love, as we mentioned earlier. One mother told me that she literally could not even touch her daughter in any way. In the midst of all of this, new and disturbing thoughts may begin to plague you. One father began to worry that his homosexual son was going to kill himself. He then became preoccupied with his wife's health and with how his son's declaration of his sexuality was affecting her adversely. He often described this effect in exaggerated terms. For some parents this stage of grief even triggers suicidal feelings within them.

Many behaviors are directed toward keeping things the way they used to be, or at least the way the parents thought they were and wanted them to be. Parents rush in with suggestions, from thinly veiled to overt coercion, bribery, or earnest and open discussion as attempts to fix it somehow. "You must see a psychiatrist." "Have you prayed about it? If you would only start going to church and truly accept Christ." Parents may play on the child's sympathy or sense of loyalty to the family, or may threaten withdrawal of financial support. A father and mother who were referred to me had already disinherited their thirty-year-old son.

All this may sound harsh and hard on parents. It is not meant to be. First, it *is* reporting actual and somewhat frequent behavior. Second, it is understandable as being among the *early* reactions. You *do* want to try to fix it, to *change* your son or daughter to be heterosexual, to marry, to have children. Because parents' lives have been so radically altered by this experience, they are often angry and they often feel panic.

Parents may spend a lot of time daydreaming about when their child was younger, looking at pictures or toys or clothing or awards that remind them of earlier and happier days before their dreams were shattered.

The third stage of grief, as described by Parkes, is *disorganization and despair.* His description of it compared to one's response to death has similarities here, too. This stage begins with a diminishing of the intensity and frequency of the weeping, anger, guilt, confusion, and other behaviors of the second stage. The child may make some efforts to please the parents by going to a counselor or attending church, but more often than not this fails to accomplish what the parents want. The truth of their child's homosexuality gradually sinks in, and they begin to accept it as the way it is going to be. They may form an uneasy truce with the child, but unhappiness, awkwardness with each other, tension within and between the parents, and between them and their son or daughter still remain. They give up most of the attempts to recapture the past, but they have not yet accomplished the central task of developing their future as persons and as a family in the light of this new reality. They don't think much about the future, and when they do, it seems dark and dreary.

The final stage of grief Parkes calls *reorganization.* The attempts to hold on to the past and to the last vestiges of hope that the homosexual son or daughter will miraculously change disappear and the situation is seen for what it truly is. Genuine reconciliation may begin to take place as relationships between the parents and between them and their son or daughter begin to improve. Even though the parents do not necessarily approve of the child's behavior, they love and accept the child. The parents can look to their own future with revised self-images, with self-esteem instead of self-blame and self-pity. They have expressed and worked through anger; their sadness is lessened, although it may persist and be felt from time to time; any depression that parents have felt over this situation is gone. Just as the parents' reactions in the other stages described here must not be interpreted as being too "bad," too pessimistic, the description of this stage must not be seen as always too "good," too optimistic. All parent–child problems and all marriage problems that may have arisen during this time are frequently not completely solved. Disappointment and some sadness may never go away. But there is a basic reorganization of individual and family life if the earlier stages of the process have been handled well.

Like the death of a family member, the information that a son or daughter is homosexual also has the initial impact of changing family members' perceptions of one another, and therefore it changes and is a threat to the family system itself. Not only do parents respond differently to that particular person, but often tension develops between the parents themselves. Occasionally, the death of a child will immediately draw the husband and wife closer to each other. Many times, however, barriers arise between them. Individuals in a family grieve differently. Some want to talk about it; others don't want to mention the person who died. Some recover more quickly than others. It becomes difficult to understand one another. They pull away from each other, even sometimes resent each other, as severe readjustments in their own relationship are made necessary. Needs that were formerly met by the presence of the child are obviously not met any longer. Parents look to each other to meet those needs at a time when each of them is obviously less capable of doing so, and this produces frustration, tension, anger. Even when the parents have similar experiences, each may react differently. One may have outbursts of temper. The other may withdraw. Communication is made extremely difficult under these circumstances, so that even many of the usual, everyday decisions are more difficult to make and the ordinary conflicts difficult to resolve. The difficulty is increased if only one parent or only a sibling knows about the gay or lesbian family member. The "secret" must be carefully guarded. The free expression of feelings and open communication is inhibited, and tension is increased.

Something of the same reaction may occur in the situation we are talking about here, with a few additional complications. One parent may blame the other, or they both may get into the blaming game; one may be fairly understanding of the child and the other condemnatory and angry, neither spouse then understanding or supporting the other. Earlier unresolved issues, such as previous losses or marital stress, may be stirred up by the pain and anxiety and increased need this present situation produces. If this happens, parents need not be surprised or dismayed. It does not necessarily mean the end of things for them. If they realize that it is fairly common that such tensions arise, they will have greater understanding of themselves and each other and thus be better prepared to work on the realistic differences between them at this time.

It is essential to recognize that a family is not just a group of individuals who have emotional ties to one another. Rather, those individuals comprise a single system, with each person having developed, often unconsciously, characteristic behaviors that they believe will assure their needs are met most effectively. The purpose of a human system is to meet as fully as possible the needs of every member and to maintain the life of the system itself. Obviously, even in the best of systems these two goals may occasionally be in tension with one another. But if either one of the goals rather consistently predominates to the detriment of the other, the system becomes dysfunctional. Very often the discovery that a family member is lesbian or gay produces a disruption of the basic family system. Some families are more capable than others of handling this situation. Those who have extreme difficulty would find it very helpful to consult a well-trained family therapist. Some clergy have such training, but many do not.

Of course, there are notable differences between the experience of "We've lost our child" when the discovery is made that a child is gay or lesbian and many other situations of grief. In death, for instance, there is a body to help make the fact of the loss more concrete: viewing the body, having the funeral, observing the burial. In contrast, the homosexual son or daughter is still there, continuing to stimulate the many feelings and the confusion. As one person said, "He looks and sounds like the child of ours whom we've known for so long; we share common memories. But this person is different, and I behave differently toward him."

At the time of death, church members and other friends and neighbors visit. They are with us as we weep and talk about our loss. They are understanding and supportive, since death is universal. They join with us in the common language and acts of the funeral service as together we remember the one we love in the midst of our worship of God. All this is sustaining and strengthening for us.

Discovering that a son or daughter is homosexual is seldom a public event. Other persons are often not in a position to know. Usually parents do not want to tell anyone. Even when they do tell one or two trusted friends, these friends sometimes feel very ill at ease and don't know how to respond, especially at first. Others who may find out about the situation tend *not* to come and offer themselves in this time of need because of their own discomfort.

When they are grieving over a death, people often feel more a part of a community of faith and support; however, when they have discovered that a son or daughter is homosexual, they usually feel more isolated and are left alone within their families to experience in their various ways their burden, guilt, shame, anger, disruption, confusion. In fact, one mother expressed her feelings in this way: "I'd rather he *was* dead. If my child had died, his potential and dignity and morality would have been intact and I could have been proud. Now I am shamed with how he has turned out."

Family members' (usually especially parents' or spouses') first reactions to the discovery that a son or a husband is gay are rendered much more poignant, more fearful, more complicated by the existence of the terrible disease of AIDS and the toll it has taken and continues to take. Since the mid-1980s most parents who discover a son is gay not only must begin to deal with their responses to that knowledge, with all that entails, but they may also think fearfully, "Does he have AIDS?" Only a few parents seem to ask that question directly at first, but the unspoken fear is there. Very frequently, it is one of the first questions to a gay husband. If the gay person has been tested for HIV and the results are negative, he often states this to the family member(s) fairly soon, hoping to diminish their anxiety. Some have not been tested. They do not want to know. Different gays and different families handle this quandary in different ways.

It is small comfort to family members to realize that persons other than gays contract the virus in a number of other ways. The disease is still associated with gay sexual activity, and this is *your* son or brother or spouse. Many gays who contracted the virus years ago are now having the disease of AIDS itself, and many are dying. The prospect of this experience for a family is terrifying. Remember, however, many gays are not HIV-positive, and some who are positive have lived with it for many years but they do not have the disease of AIDS.

If your son reveals that he is suffering from AIDS, don't allow your other reactions to this revelation to blot out your realization that he is in great need of your love and support in his illness, his fear of suffering and death, although any denial on your part of his being gay may also include a denial of the illness. Many gays, if they have the illness or even if they are HIV-positive, do not initially admit this fact to family members. They are usually afraid enough of your reactions to their being gay without adding on this tragic news. Some do not want to burden you with this reality now as they try to protect you as long as possible. After all, they reason, you have enough to deal with just with the discovery (or confirmation) that he is gay.

Some parents have the difficult experience of discovering that their son is homosexual only after he has a series of serious illnesses and begins to deteriorate, and it becomes apparent that he has AIDS and is dying. The shock of this situation is at times overwhelming.

What can you do in this time of need? Some families seem to have been able to muster their combined personal resources, talk and cry together, and handle it themselves. Even these, though, usually talk with physicians and nurses who specialize in the treatment of AIDS, most likely with those who are caring for their son (or other family member). Some read all they can find out about the virus and the disease. They gain both knowledge and support from these professionals and from their reading. Other families talk with trusted friends, a minister or priest, a mental health professional, especially one who is known to have experience in helping families deal with this situation. In most cities the local medical and psychological associations can usually provide the names of these professionals. Some larger hospitals also have AIDS chaplains who can be reached through the Office of the Chaplain (or Department of Pastoral Care). Others who live in or near large cities have found it helpful to contact an agency that specializes in working with people with AIDS and their families (AIDS Interfaith Network, for example, or others). Counselors are available in many agencies, as are family support groups.

If you choose to go to a minister or priest, you need to remember that they are also people. They differ from one another, and they may differ from you. What they believe about homosexuality depends on their interpretation of the Bible and on their variety of feelings about this sexual orientation and behavior. It may be confusing or even frustrating to you if the minister's views on homosexuality and homosexual persons vary from yours. This is not the major issue, however. A minister whose views differ from yours may still be able to love you and your son or daughter, listen to you, help you clarify your own feelings, and help you communicate more effectively with one another. In this process, you can be helped significantly.

Nevertheless, if you discover that the minister or priest is uptight emotionally about the matter and, therefore, not able to listen attentively and communicate understanding, if the minister is condemnatory of homosexual persons, then the goals of emotional expression, mutual understanding, and reconciliation that you desire for yourselves and your family will probably not be achieved. If you realize this after your initial conversation, you would do well to find someone else to talk to. You must consider your own needs, and not the program of a minister who does not have the sensitivity to help you discover and work out your goals.

Seeing the similarities between the grief that is in reaction to death and the complex reactions to the disclosure that your son or daughter is homosexual provides a perspective for you that can help you understand more adequately the experience you are going through. It assures you that what you are experiencing within yourselves as individuals and between each other and your family is not abnormal. A combination of these feelings and behaviors is to be expected. You can prepare yourselves to tolerate some of them, because after a while they will diminish and some will even vanish. You can allow yourselves to feel some of the emotions deeply; in fact, you *need* to allow yourselves to feel them, rather than repress them and pretend they are not there. You can push yourselves to talk openly and honestly with one another within the family as a way of resolving some of the issues. Although you may hesitate for a number of reasons, you can talk with a minister or other professional counselor about yourselves and your situation. You are reminded that your experiences are a part of a process that you must go through all the way, and not a situation in which you can successfully bypass important tasks and skip stages. It will take time.

Finally, it is important to remember Paul's call in 2 Corinthians to all Christians to join in "the ministry of reconciliation," the central duty, yes, opportunity, of us all in all circumstances. In this situation, as in times of grief over death, Paul's words in Romans continue to ring true, that nothing "will be able to separate us from the love of God in Christ Jesus our Lord" (Rom. 8:39). *Nothing!* God has not abandoned you, although you may feel that way; nor has God abandoned your son or daughter or other family member, although you may at first interpret it that way. Rather, in this situation as in all situations, God continues to be present and to work with you toward fulfilling promises of a new future for you made originally in the covenant with the Jews and renewed in the event of Jesus Christ.

3   *Is Our Child Really Gay?*

But wait a minute! Perhaps we have reacted too quickly. I have been writing as though it is a foregone conclusion that the young person or young adult *is* homosexual. Often parents respond prematurely in this same way. They hear from someone else that their child has been caught "messing around" with someone of the same sex. Or they have noticed that the child hasn't dated in the usual sense, prefers to be with peers of the same sex, or has a "special friend" of the same sex. Or the son or daughter confides in them a deep concern about feeling sexually attracted to someone of the same sex. Or the child uses the actual words, "Mom, Dad, I'm gay (or lesbian)."

A frequent tendency of parents in most of these instances is to leap immediately into the midst of shock and denial, with the unconscious assumption that any one of these disclosures means that their child actually *is* lesbian or gay. They automatically deny that it's true; they try to gloss it over; they don't want to talk about it. They have some of the feelings that were described in chapter 2, when all the while they may be misjudging the true nature of the situation. They may be going through all this unnecessarily and may say things they later regret, or at the very least they fail to get the information that is necessary in order for them to know more clearly what is actually going on in the life of their son or daughter and what he or she is trying to communicate to them. They miss their opportunity to be as helpful to their child as they might be.

The point is, the young person *may* be homosexual, or may *not* be. People mean different things by the word *gay* or *lesbian* or *homosexual.* The fact that persons use it about themselves does not necessarily mean that they are giving a technically accurate description of their condition. Also, the same or similar feelings or behavior in persons of different ages may be related to different things going on in their lives. All this needs to be explored and not reacted to prematurely with denial, panic, anger, or condemnation. It is important for parents to avoid certain extremes of reaction. On the one hand, they may fail to take seriously feelings or behavior that are genuinely disturbing to the young person; on the other, they may overreact by taking too seriously that which may not be particularly troubling to the young person or which is not necessarily proof that the person is really homosexual.

A very good friend called me from another city years ago to ask me if I would be willing to talk with his daughter, who was seventeen. She had told her parents that she was lesbian and in love with a woman just a few years older than she. The parents were stunned but were able to talk reasonably and reassuringly with her. Of course, I was willing to talk with her and she picked up the phone. We spoke for perhaps forty-five minutes and agreed to be in touch with each other within the next week or two. She called back later and again we had another forty-five-minute conversation. It sounded to me as if she perhaps were lesbian, although the reason she lacked dating experience with boys was that she had rarely been invited out and she experienced homosexual feelings only within the last year or two. Over the next two or three years in occasional conversations the parents reported that she was still in the same relationship. For various reasons, after that, we were not in touch with each other for about fifteen years. Just recently, though, her father and I were able to visit with each other. I asked him about his daughter. He said that the relationship with the woman had concluded quite a long while ago, that his daughter had married and had a child, and that she reported not being sexually attracted to women.

The parents had taken their daughter seriously. They had not tried to force her to change. They had not condemned her. They had asked her to talk with me and she did. The parents, while concerned, allowed her to be who she was at the time, and with the increasing maturity of years and increased social experience, she moved toward who she really was sexually.

This is not to suggest that when a teenager declares herself or himself to be lesbian or gay, if the parents just keep their cool, after a few years their child will become a heterosexual adult. Not at all! It is to suggest that *sometimes* this is the case, but either way, the parents need to take their children seriously, sensitively explore the children's experiences, and ask them to talk with a competent and trusted professional about it.

A contrast is seen in the poignancy with which a young man in his late twenties spoke of his parents' casual disregard when in his middle teens he told them of his sexual feelings toward other boys. Having grown up in his home, his church, his society, he had inevitably made the same assumptions about his own sexuality that others had made—that is, that he would be heterosexual, marry, and have children—and he had assimilated some of the same negative feelings toward homosexuality that the people around him shared. Now his own self-image was being shaken, and he felt deeply worried and very bad about himself. His mother responded to his painful opening of himself with, "Oh, it's just a phase. Don't worry about it. You'll get over it." Rather than being relieved, he felt as if he were not being taken seriously. It felt like a rejection of who he was. It was to him as though she were making light of his agonizing struggle. Many feelings and some homosexual relations after that, he finally found his way to a psychiatrist's office—the wrong person for him, and too late. He has had to go through years of dealing with his bad feelings about himself and his difficult efforts to work out his identity for the most part alone, certainly without his parents' or a sensitive and competent professional's aid. He is gay today and now feels good about himself. But it was a long and painful and lonely journey. Parents can be more helpful to their children than this. They need not lose years of a relationship.

On the other hand, I have known parents of some fourteen-year-old children who reported homosexual feelings or instances of mutual masturbation with a peer. These parents dealt with them as if these early teenagers were adults who had been homosexually promiscuous. Their parents' emotional and behavioral overreaction has confused the children, has had the effect of either creating or reinforcing their bad feelings about themselves, and has cut off what might have been a close and truly helpful relationship between parents and children.

What do parents need to know, and what can they do?

First, what is homosexuality anyway? My purpose at this point is merely to attempt to give a definition. In chapter 8 I shall say much more about the nature of the condition and describe the different theories regarding the causes of the sexual orientation. Now let's just take a look at some of the definitions that have been proposed.

A pamphlet published by the Sex Information and Education Council of the U.S. states this: "Homosexuality refers to emotional attachments involving sexual attraction and/or overt sexual relations between individuals—male or female—of the same sex."[1] Very simple. But does that mean, then, that any person of any age who at any time has sexual feelings toward someone of the same sex or who has sexual relations with a person of the same sex is gay or lesbian? No, not at all. Not so simple then. The definition enables us to say what homosexual feelings and homosexual behavior are. It does not tell us who *is* a homosexual person. Human beings, and our lives together, are far more complex than that.

The Public Affairs pamphlet dealing with this subject says, "Homosexuality means sexual attraction to persons of the same sex as oneself, whether male or female," which is the same definition as the one above, but a second paragraph seems to sharpen this statement considerably by adding that the term refers "to persons who are exclusively or primarily attracted to members of their own sex, and who enter into sexual and affectional relations with them."[2] This latter statement is more helpful because it doesn't label people who have occasional homosexual feelings as *being* homosexual, because this is not necessarily so. It seems to allow for temporary situational forces that lead to such feelings and/or behavior. It also makes a very important distinction between feelings and behavior. However, this definition does not account for the different ages of persons or their stages of development.

More accurate is Rosser's generic definition that "sexual orientation refers to *adult* stable sexual attractions, desires, fantasies, and expressions toward other adult men and women."[3] This definition allows for adolescent confusion, for exploration, or for transitional relationships. It suggests that a judgment as to sexual orientation during that time can only be tentative. However, the definition does not seem to allow for the fact that adults may in fact have an attraction to, a desire for, or fantasies about persons of the same sex but not engage in explicitly sexual relations with them (as might a priest who wants to remain celibate or has other religious or practical reasons, or those who are gay or lesbian in *orientation* but are married to a person of the other sex and are sexually faithful to his or her spouse).

Rosser's definition, and others very much like it, allows for the reality of the complexity of factors that go into determining the choice of sexual objects, and the human being has the capacity for quite a variety of these. Different childrearing methods, different environmental situations, and other factors lead young and mid-adolescents (eleven or twelve to fifteen or sixteen years of age), in particular, and sometimes even older adolescents or adults either to experiment with different sexual objects or to have a relationship with someone of the same sex exclusively or predominately for a brief period of time. For a young or mid-teenager to have sexual feelings for someone of the same sex does not necessarily mean that this person *is* a homosexual or is destined to become lesbian or gay. It *may* mean that, but often it does not. These feelings and, on occasion, even behavior in an older person do not necessarily mean that this person *is* homosexual. Many persons at certain times in their lives, or even from time to time throughout their lives, may be sexually aroused by a person of the same sex, but their predominant feelings and exclusive or primary sexual expression are heterosexual.

From time to time we hear the term *bisexual* used. If this word is used by a family member to describe herself or himself, the shock to the family is just as great as if the person had said that he or she is gay or lesbian, and, if anything, it is more confusing. What such a declaration means, among other things, is that she or he does have sexual feelings for and is attracted to persons of the same sex and may have had sexual relationships with them, yet may also have felt affection for and had sexual relationships with someone of the other sex. For parents and other family members, the basic reactions and issues are still the same. Realizing that the person may also be attracted to members of the other sex doesn't seem to ameliorate the dismay at the news of his or her homosexuality.

There is lack of agreement among professionals in the field of human sexuality regarding numerous issues relating to bisexuality; there is also lack of clarity within many persons who claim that *bisexual* describes themselves. A simple definition—offered by William Stanton and perhaps as accurate as any could be—is that "bisexuals are persons attracted to people of either sex. They may or may not have had overt sexual activity with either or both sexes."[4] Stanton clarifies that one must take account of the distinctions between behavior, fantasy, and emotional attachments. Only one of these may be present, or two, or all in considerably varying degrees.

Although I make no claim to be an expert in this area, putting together all the information that I have accumulated from talking with persons about their sex lives, their conflicts, and confusion and all that I have read and discussed with a psychiatrist, I have found that by far the majority of those who say that they are bisexual have a clear, distinct heterosexual or homosexual orientation. The fantasies about and attractions to someone other than those of the primary orientation, the relationships and explicit sex with them are more situational in nature. Dynes indicates that most people who claim to be bisexual are more properly classified as either homosexual or heterosexual.[5]

Within the family it seems to serve no useful purpose to argue the point. Such arguments or attempts to push the person toward a commitment to exclusive heterosexuality will be counterproductive. They will serve only to divert parents and other family members from an awareness of their internal reactions and everyone from their goal of reconciliation with one another.

Another expression in common use, "the homosexual lifestyle," is intended to be descriptive but is in fact inaccurate and confusing. Have you ever heard people talking about "the heterosexual lifestyle?" Then why in the name of common sense is the term "the homosexual lifestyle" in such widespread use? These expressions would seem to suggest that only two lifestyles are available to human beings and that we can choose either one we want. In fact, numerous lifestyles are available to people, and these are accessible to both homosexual and heterosexual persons. A lifestyle is relatively freely chosen, and under a variety of circumstances people can and do change their lifestyles. Homosexuality and heterosexuality are *sexual orientations,* not lifestyles, and they are *not* relatively freely chosen. They should not be referred to as anything other than sexual orientations that are the result, primarily, if not exclusively, of forces beyond a person's conscious control (see chapter 8).

These distinctions that I have detailed here are important because similar feelings, similar behaviors, and similar words on the part of different children of different ages and in varying situations discussing themselves with their parents may have a variety of meanings. Therefore, the discussion should focus on the specific feelings and behaviors that the teenager or adult child has and not on general terms.

What are some helpful ways to respond?

First and foremost, don't dodge the issue. The subject may

come up in a number of ways. So far in this book we have tended to assume that the young person or young adult who wants to come out has probably dropped clues to the parents from time to time. Possibly, the parents were able to hear and understand, or possibly they were not. But finally the child tells the parent in some reasonably direct way.

Most of the time they do so because they want to have an open and honest relationship with their parents. But in some instances, the concrete words will come out unexpectedly as an expression of real hostility in the context of an argument. Numerous gay persons report that often they have been on the verge of blurting their news out in anger, and they have had to bite their tongues to keep from it. Sometimes biting the tongue doesn't work and they say it. It sounds harsh. "You're still trying to run my life. You've always done it, and look what kind of job you did. You've produced a queer!" "You think you're so good and know it all. What would you think if you knew I was gay?"

Whatever the circumstances, the reactions discussed in chapters 2 and 3 are stirred up. But to hear it in an argument or a call from someone else worsens the situation. Regardless, the basic task is still the same: to talk about it in detail. If it occurs during an argument, the immediate anger has to be dealt with before the substance of the matter can be discussed in any detail. But then the parent, if the son or daughter has not already done so, must initiate the discussion. "Let's talk specifically about what you said about your being gay." Or if the parents hear it from someone else, it is imperative that they initiate the conversation with their child: "I just talked to ———, and he said that you were homosexual. That was a terrible shock to me. What about it? Tell me honestly about yourself." Even in shocking and emotional circumstances, the potential remains for serious discussion with one another, and it is essential that this take place.

Please don't misunderstand. I am not suggesting that you can always remain calm, cool, and collected. I am not saying, "Don't *feel* anything; just talk rationally." No one can advise concerning another person's feelings. Nearly all parents are going to experience one or several of the feelings we have already described. If you have strong feelings, and you probably have or will, accept them for what they are. Express them in some way verbally. Tell your son or daughter how you feel. Weep if you feel like it. You can't immediately control *what* feelings arise. But your behavior can be reasonably well under control. Even though you may tremble, cry some, feel very angry, or have other reactions, you can still carry on the conversation (or more likely, the series of conversations) that will be necessary.

To begin with, remember that your child is having some strong feelings, too. Even when the words come out in anger, your child usually cares very deeply how you react and has some fear about your response. It is likely that your child has thought about telling you for months and even years, mentally reviewed it, planned it, and then postponed it because of great anxiety.

So now that you are talking about it, however unpleasant it is for you, you need to stay with it. First of all, listen. Invite your child to tell what she or he is willing to tell. Then listen. This first task is absolutely necessary: to try to understand the experience of your child. This is not the same thing as immediately "approving" or agreeing to it; you are merely trying to understand the past and present experiences of this person.

Ask questions that can help you understand, trying not to be too invasive of very personal experiences. Make summarizing statements that either communicate that you *are* understanding or perhaps that you are not and that you need more clarity.

Help your son or daughter review the history of his or her experiences. Ask, "When and how did you first become aware of these feelings? What was it like for you? Has it always been clear to you, or have there been times of confusion and conflicts? What feelings have you had about yourself?" In the process of gaining information for yourself, try to move toward understanding, thereby communicating love and support to your son or daughter. As you listen with all seriousness, you may also be helping your child to clarify his or her own experiences. Regardless of whatever feelings you may be having, you are in fact helping to bring yourself closer to your son or daughter.

Talk about why you are discussing this right now: "What were your reasons for initiating this with me?" Or "You were really mad at me when you said that. I wish it could have come out in some other way, but here it is. Besides being mad at me, is there some other reason you've told me about it?" Or "I'm sorry I had to get information like this from someone else. Tell me what's been going on with you and what has stood in the way of your speaking to me about it."

Throughout this discussion, be honest with your son or daughter.

You too are having painful and conflicting thoughts and feelings, and it is important for you to express them: "This is very difficult for me. It really hurts." "I find myself feeling guilty and blaming myself but feeling mad at you at the same time." "I'm trying, but I find it very difficult to understand."

Because you too are a person with feelings, it will be more helpful to the relationship to express them than to try to pretend you don't have them. However, it is certainly possible that the strength of your feelings and your confusion may lead you to say things that you later (a few minutes, hours, days) wish you hadn't said. You may feel bad about it, and the words may have angered or hurt your child, but you can always take words back or, at least, apologize for them. In this we are all in the same human boat. If this happens, it is important to express clearly to your son or daughter what it is like for you. "When I said ———, I was really furious at you (or "feeling panicky," or "devastated,"), and I am really sorry that I said it or said it the way I did. It expressed my real feelings at the time, but it is not the main way I view you and feel about you. Would you try to understand and forgive me for it?"

Keep in mind during your initial conversations that wide differences are possible in the meanings of words, feeling, and behaviors of children depending upon their ages and the circumstances, as we discussed earlier. Keeping in mind these differences, try to discover what your child is really trying to communicate to you and what the child wants from you at this time. Ask, "When you use the word 'gay' (or 'homosexual' or 'bisexual') about yourself, what specifically do you mean?" "You say that you and ——— did this together. How long has it been going on? Is it something you have done just once or twice, or has it been often? Does that mean that you are really sexually attracted to that person and only to persons of the same sex, or have you also been attracted to someone of the other sex?" Or with an older child ask, "Are you in love, and/or are you living with someone now?" To repeat an earlier point, even though your son or daughter is talking with you about some homosexual feelings or behavior and about confusion concerning himself or herself, he or she may not in fact be homosexual. Or he or she may be. It is very important to make these distinctions and discover what the reality is.

Again, we realize that we are proposing a dialogue take place that is extremely difficult for parents, and usually for the child too. You may not want to ask. You may be afraid to hear the answer. Your son or daughter may not really want to respond to you. But the subject is up and out, and the reality of it needs to be clarified. To do so, certain minimal information is necessary. Of course, questions asking for much minute detail should be avoided. The young person or adult has a right to privacy about intimate matters, just as you yourself do.

The conversation may lead to open discussion about what your son or daughter expects of you. This knowledge can help you shape your responses and once again assist in maintaining your relationship at a particularly difficult time.

Especially with young and mid-teens, and occasionally with older teens and those in their early twenties, a son's or daughter's real desire in talking to you may be only to gain an increased understanding of herself or himself: "What do these feelings, this behavior, mean about *me*? I'm confused about *myself*. Why am I like this? What is my future going to be? I feel so bad about myself." The young persons may or may not want to change their feelings and behavior; but their fundamental project is self-understanding. Realizing that they have their parents' genuine support at this time is extremely important for them. If they gain significant self-understanding, although it may not make them "change into heterosexuals," some of them may discover that they are not truly homosexual. At any rate, self-understanding, insight, a good self-concept are essential to any human being. This is the beginning point. Most teenagers will need their parents' guidance. Where do they get this kind of assistance? Some may come from parents themselves through just such discussions as we are describing here, but much help can come from talking with a minister or other professional counselor. "Aye, there's the rub." As a matter of fact, there are a couple of rubs.

The first one is how the parents make the suggestion. If it is in panic and anger, with bribes or threats, the young person may rebel and refuse to go for the help that is needed and, quite often, genuinely wanted. A better response of the parents is this: "It sounds as if you are very confused about the whole matter yourself and feel bad about yourself, and that you are really asking for some way to understand yourself better. Also, although we want to continue to talk with you ourselves, there are probably some things you may not feel free to say to us but probably could to someone else. What do you think about our trying to find someone you could talk to?"

The second rub is selecting the best person to talk to. It may be that your minister or some other minister is a good choice. For young people to whom the Christian faith is meaningful, who have had or still have some ties to the church, there can be real advantages in talking with a minister. But as I mentioned earlier, how the minister views homosexuality and especially homosexual persons, how he or she feels about them, and whether the minister has training in counseling are key factors that need to be considered. Can the minister understand people who are different from himself or herself, be nonjudgmental, work helpfully with them without being overly anxious, be compassionate and not authoritarian? These are especially critical factors.

Interestingly, more than one gay person has reported to me that ministers with whom they have sought counseling have not been openly condemning; rather they have tended to pass off too easily what the young person is telling them. They may say, for instance, "I've known your family and I've known you for so many years, and you all are good solid people. Many people have these feelings. It's just a phase. You'll get over it." While these statements may in fact describe some young persons, they clearly are not true for all and can be hurtfully misleading. To respond too quickly in this way, even though it might be the case, fails to take the young person's disclosure seriously. Three possibilities can account for this type of response. First, the minister may have little awareness of what homosexuality really is. Second, the response may be prompted by the minister's own denial and inability and unwillingness to deal seriously with this person about this issue. Third, the minister's reasoning may follow this line: "Homosexuality is depravity. I know you and you are not depraved. Therefore, it's impossible for you to be homosexual." Beginning with false assumptions, such ministers can reach a conclusion with tragic implications for the person asking for help.

Nevertheless, numerous young people and adults who have been confused or disturbed by their homosexual feelings and behavior, who have been trying to clarify their sexual identity, or who have been afraid to tell their parents (or *have* told them but with distressing results) have been able to talk with their minister or another minister and, in doing so, have found compassion and personal support and gained clarity for themselves. Even ministers who interpret the Bible as condemning homosexuality and/or homosexual acts, and who themselves see it as sinful, can respond as compassionate human beings and good listeners, providing accurate feedback and facilitating the person's self-exploration and decision-making. Parents, too, have received help from such ministers.

What about psychiatrists or psychologists or other well-trained professional counselors? Their ability to be helpful also varies. Don't depend on the yellow pages. Find out. Avoid the two extremes: those who start from the premise that all homosexuals should be changed into heterosexuals and those who too easily and quickly say, "You are okay just like you are. You just need to feel better about yourself." Select instead one who always begins by helping the person to explore feelings, background, relationships, conflicts, needs, the meaning of behavior. This kind of counselor, on the basis of such work, will then help the person set goals and assist in the achievement of them.

Some young people, especially those who are in their twenties or older, realize that ultimately the parents may find out about their sexual orientation one way or another. Therefore, they decide that it is only right for the parents to hear it from them directly. Even when tension, uneasiness, or even anger and alienation exist between them, the young people want to establish a better relationship with their parents. When they do decide to talk with their parents about being gay or lesbian, it is primarily to share a significant area of their lives, to reduce the tension of living a lie with them (although obviously other tensions are usually created), and, they hope, to be accepted as they are as a member of the family. Even if the child is older, it doesn't necessarily mean that she or he has no confusion or problems or low self-esteem, but by this time some of them have had one or more real love attachments, and they may actually be living with someone at the time. The gay life is already well established, and they have no intent to change.

There are several things parents should avoid if they can. One is the use of threats, bribery, or pleading in trying to appeal to their son's or daughter's guilt as a means of getting the person to change, to stop doing this. As we have emphasized, the parent will probably be feeling shock, confusion, a sense of panic, anger, and for this reason they are likely to say all sorts of things. It is all right for parents to express those feelings, but they can do so in ways that allow them to move into the more constructive conversations that we have described and given examples of. Meaningful conversation cannot continue if a parent bans a son or daughter from the home with a mandate not to return until he or she has changed. Forcing a child to see a minister or a psychiatrist under threat will not bring about what the parents desire. Many young people have felt even more alienated and angry as a result of their parents' not-too-subtle bribes and bargaining. This is not to suggest that parents should eliminate earnest conversation regarding what they would like to see the child do so long as these desires are expressed in clear and straightforward terms and are understood simply for what they are—the parents' desires and best advice.

It is also important to avoid the suggestion that meeting the "right" person will correct the situation. All too often advice like this is offered to a son "You just need to date more. If you could only find a good woman, it would be different. If you only had a woman to make love to, you wouldn't have these feelings any longer." And the same to a daughter about "just needing the right man." Too much pain and damage has occurred as a result of advice like this. Many young people genuinely want to please their parents. They may therefore try the suggested courses of action, all too frequently to their own and someone else's detriment. Especially hurtful have been those situations when, in confusion and under parental pressure, a homosexual person marries someone of the other sex, only to have it all fall apart later.

For any parent who has just discovered that a child is homosexual, the first order of business is to work on the quality of their own being, to be someone who can still love and communicate even in the midst of a shocking and painful experience. The crucial question is, Can you be who you are and still be the loving parents of children who are as *they* are, even when they are quite different from you?

4 Where Does the Fault Belong?

If your child is gay or lesbian, when the initial shock of disclosure or discovery has somewhat abated and the period of denial is over, it is quite normal for you to begin to have some very angry feelings. Sometimes these feelings come out in a blast at the child who has revealed this hidden self to you. Sometimes the anger is not available for expression, and the feeling that you are most aware of is pain that is experienced physically as well as emotionally. You may also have feelings of depression that come from held-in anger. It takes so much energy to contain it that the result is fatigue and often feelings of tension as well.

After Jan told me she was gay, I was numb for days. Then I began to clean my house like I had never cleaned house before. I was out in the back yard one morning hanging up some curtains I had washed. I was jabbing the clothespins on real hard. When I came into the house my husband said I should look in the mirror, that I looked furious. I did and he was right. I began to cry, really hard sobs, and beat the kitchen table with my fists. It really was good to get that out. It surprised me that I felt stronger.

Initially, parents often feel that it is not safe or appropriate to allow their angry feelings to be directed openly toward the son or daughter who has apparently chosen to be different. So they tend to displace much of that negative feeling onto "evil" influences around that person and outside the home. Even in the midst of a great deal of hurt and anger and disappointment many parents quite naturally tend to rush to the defense of their children. The younger the child, the more often this is so.

Knowledge of the fact that a son or daughter is lesbian or gay is often experienced as a loss of the total person. Therefore, the anger accompanying that experience makes you feel as if someone or some group has taken your son or daughter from you. If it happens when the child is older, more mature, or a young adult, the parents are more likely to believe that their child simply did not resist temptation and therefore took himself or herself away from them. The thinking here often still tends to be focused on the influences of persons outside the family, however. The content of parents' thoughts can be very vengeful. This is all part of our very common human reluctance to let go of those we love—to lose them either to death or to a direction we don't want them to go. You are not "bad" human beings to have such angry, hate-filled thoughts. To think and feel is not necessarily to act, and this is an important distinction to make at this time. Your anger is simply a part of the process, and this, too, passes with time, especially if you continue to express the feelings and confusion by talking with your child, other family members, a competent pastoral counselor, or some other caregiver.

We human beings have a great need for reasons and explanations, to find meanings for events. Your speculation about how it all happened—that your homosexual son or daughter became so—may have many elements of blaming. Blaming is part of the search for meaning, and it is common to want to thrust on to another the responsibility for an event that we experience as hurtful. When we are hurt and angry we want to accuse and blame, and frequently we want very much to punish whatever or whomever we have decided is the cause of our pain and loss. To discover a cause other than oneself does give us a temporary sense that we now understand how it happened.

There has to be a reason that this absolutely normal little boy has grown up to be gay. He had a happy, uneventful childhood. He did not have any trauma in his young life that hundreds of kids haven't had, too. We were reasonably good parents. All I can think of is that he went to a big university far away from home. He was young and vulnerable and lonely. He was taken advantage of. That university had a responsibility to provide a decent place for shy kids to meet and get to know each other. They are thrown on their own at such a tender age. We trusted that school and it was a terrible mistake. Too much sexual propaganda is allowed.

The intensity of feeling that accompanies blaming can be dismaying, even frightening. Parents speak of wanting to attack verbally, and sometimes even physically, those whom they believe influenced or caused their son or daughter to become this person they didn't want a child of theirs to be. They imagine and fantasize about harsh accusations and punishments of those they want to hold responsible. One father who felt very strongly about his thirty-something-year-old son's telling them recently that he was gay still allowed his son to visit, although he felt angry, betrayed, confused, awkward, and tense with him. But this father threatened to shoot any of his gay friends if he brought them home with him.

It's the rotten newspapers and TV. They glorify sin and immorality. Can't turn on the set without some "expert" talking about how many people are acting in what I consider sinful ways—and that makes it okay for everybody. Now they seem to be pushing this gay and lesbian stuff on us all the time. The media should have some sense of responsibility for upgrading the moral fiber of this country. What chance do parents have to raise kids decently with all that corruption? Sometimes, especially right now, I'd like to get my hands on the guys who allow that stuff on the air. They'd have another think coming!

Personally, I believe that many current radio or TV talk shows do seem to have gone wild in their presentation of strange relationships and bizarre behaviors, including much sexual behavior. I can't help but believe that this supersaturation of the airways has a noxious influence on values in general, but it does not *cause* anyone to be lesbian or gay.

Another group that is blamed not so much for *influencing* the young as for *not* influencing them at all is the church, particularly that segment of the church labeled liberal. The criticism often is leveled at the so-called permissiveness perceived in some theological teachings. A mother says:

It is clear to me that we have been betrayed by our own church. They have actually allowed groups of homosexuals to use our church building for meetings. I was against it when the deacons voted to give permission. I'm not sure I can support my church ever again because now it is a personal thing. If my son had had the clear-cut guidance of the church during his formative years, this might not have happened. Instead, doubt was planted in his mind and they encouraged a questioning of the high standards that the church ought to uphold.

Even ministers who preach about the central theme of loving and caring for one another are accused of condoning and encouraging immoral behavior when this message is related to gays and lesbians.

Yet in reality, just as many gays and lesbians attend or grow up in "conservative" churches as in the "liberal" ones. Preaching and teaching *against* homosexuality cannot be shown to reduce its occurrence. Certainly churches have a right, even an obligation, to teach and preach what they believe to be true. Children and young people need guidance and support. But neither "conservative" nor "liberal" churches *produce* the sexual orientation of lesbians and gays, nor do they *cause* or *allow* it to take place.

Yet many parents feel anger and bewilderment during this experience at what appears to be a failure of schools and churches to support and reinforce the principles to which they, the parents, adhere. Many of these parents express great helplessness and rage as they explore their memories of their children and young people in church and school.

Some parents have a profound sense of being deserted by God; in some instances this feeling is accompanied with intense anger.

All my life I have been faithful to God and my church. I have loved my family as best I knew how and saw to it that we were a praying, church-attending family. And it wasn't just show either. My daughter was a leader in the youth group from junior high on, and we all supported her. I feel God has let me down, and the ones I love. Where was God's protection for my girl? My faith is utterly destroyed. I can no longer pray; there is nothing to pray to.

This particular mother went through a deep depression and expressed much anger at what she perceived as God's letting her down by not directing her daughter in the ways she believed her daughter would find happiness. With the help of a patient and kind husband and a skilled minister she came to an acceptance of God's presence, which allowed her to find comfort again in her now-stronger faith. She grieves still for her daughter, but the relationship is open and growing.

A father casting about for the reason that his son was homosexual remembered his dislike for his son's circle of friends in grade school:

> If it hadn't been for that bunch of sissies he ran around with, none of this would have happened. I never did like any of them. They were always talking, making noise, not out playing ball every day like normal kids. Their mothers should have cut out all that artsy-craftsy stuff. My boy probably wouldn't have been in all those plays in high school if he hadn't been influenced by that gang. He could have played team sports and learned how to be a real man. That bunch of kids and their mothers ruined my son.

Organized groups of homosexuals, unorganized gay persons, people both lay and professional who have anything positive to say about homosexuals—all come in for a scathing attack by some parents. For some it appears that these groups and/or individuals encourage and promote homosexuality. In actuality, of course, the groups are organized in order to respond to the needs of persons already homosexual. To parents who are earnestly searching for reasons that their son or daughter is homosexual, the distinction may not be readily clear. There is certainly enough misinformation published and discussed that can explain why otherwise thoughtful parents could feel for a while as if their son or daughter may have been victimized and unwittingly coerced into a life he or she would not have chosen if left alone.

It can only be hoped that dialogue continues between the gay or lesbian person and the parents. As this particular phase of the grief runs its course, parents can find opportunities to explore and evaluate the groups or persons they have come to blame. Perhaps in doing so they can eliminate some of them as inappropriate targets. As these targets are eliminated, however, new ones may occur. Interspersed with this blame-placing outside the home will be blame-placing very close to home, including blaming one's spouse and oneself. This will be discussed in chapter 5.

The process of working through the various stages of this grief will include times of relief, even calm, then times of going back through some of the thoughts and feelings anew. It is hoped that this "going back" will not be a return to the same point, but the reworking of some of the same issues and feelings from a different vantage point, with some new insights. These insights are best gained by earnest, open talking with the son or daughter, understanding more clearly who they are, discussing the issues with one's husband or wife and perhaps other family members, and sometimes with trusted persons outside of the family.

5 Where Did We Go Wrong?

One of the most agonizing questions parents ask themselves when a child reveals his or her homosexuality to them is, What did I do wrong? or What did we do wrong? It is a time of searching out reasons that this event happened to this child, to this family. Was it the year he was in the nursery school when his mother worked full time? Should Dad have taken more time from his work for fishing and playing ball? Should Mom have insisted on keeping her in dresses? And don't forget "odd" Uncle Hubert. Maybe there is an inherited weakness somewhere. On whose side of the family?

The human tendency to oscillate between blame and guilt in this process is inevitable: one day "knowing" it was the way the other parent behaved toward the child and the next day "knowing" that it was neglect and carelessness on one's own part. It is not at all unusual to remember some guilt-ridden behavior of the past and decide that punishment for that is now being visited through this terrible happening.

A father confessed for the first time his heavy burden of guilt for an extramarital affair that he was involved in years earlier while he was a traveling salesman. He remembered staying away from home longer than he needed to in order to spend time with his woman friend. His preoccupation with her increasing demands for more time and finally her insistence that he leave his wife had left him with little energy for or interest in his family for about a year. He remembered vividly a scene when he had slapped his small son for demanding that he come outside and look at fireflies. He recalled with tears in his own eyes the tears in the eyes of his child. Could all this be the reason? Was this son's homosexuality his own punishment for being an unfaithful husband and neglectful father? Certainly many futile bargains are made around the themes "I will never again——if only he will change and not be homosexual anymore," or "I promise I will ——if only. . . ."

Frequently, one or both parents undertake a detailed review of the child's development since birth. Often enough some lacks are recognized as real, and they feel genuine sorrow with such a realization. It is well to remember at this time a universal truth: No parent is perfect. Mistakes made when parents are young and uninformed, often made in the context of loving care, are forgivable, and far more often than not they have not been detrimental.

Ruminations in the night are common. Often parents will lie awake hour after hour, going over the child's whole life or perhaps focusing on a few painful events. Still others may go to sleep fairly easily and then awaken in the wee small hours of the morning to remember and agonize. It is during these dark and lonely times that bitterness brews and corrodes. Anger with child, spouse, and self churns and stirs the blaming and faultfinding. The term "dark night of the soul" is certainly applicable to this stage of the process. For some there will be many repetitions of such nights, and for others they will be few or sporadic. Each parent will have his or her own timetable for this process, and the timetables of the parents and other family members will likely not coincide. It is a time to be tolerant of each other's differences and feelings and the varying intensities as well. No two persons go through any emotional experience in the same way, and the length of time it takes to get through it will also vary.

It is certainly helpful if parents at this stage can talk to each other freely and openly. In other circumstances, such as illness or bereavement, the same need to talk exists, but it is usually possible to talk feelings out with many persons. Family and friends gather around and are readily available. But parents who have found out that their son or daughter is homosexual often feel very isolated. However, for many parents clergy are a present help in time of need. In many cities groups made up of the parents of homosexual men and women, such as Parents and Friends of Lesbians and Gays, can also provide support. These groups can be very helpful as a forum to discuss feelings. But most parents of homosexuals have only each other, or think they do, and that fact puts tremendous and sometimes overwhelming pressure on the relationship. The anger can get very personal, and the blaming can sometimes be vitriolic. Other side issues typically are brought in as the conflict escalates:

You criticized every boy she ever dated. None of them was good enough for your daughter. And you told her a lot of frightening things about men. How do you think that made me feel? As a matter of fact you always put me down, and not just in front of her but in front of everyone. I've resented your treatment of me for years.

The one who is being blamed can counterattack, or withdraw in wounded silence, or courageously examine the issues that surface and allow that their own relationship is in need of help. No figures are available for the number of marriages that fail following (not as a direct result of) the revelation of the knowledge of the homosexuality of their child, but it does occur just as it does following the death of a child. The opportunity that this crisis presents (and all crises *do* present opportunities) is to look anew at the marital and family relationships and do some long overdue evaluating. Where there is openness to change, there is life and possibility for the future. Talking it out is the way to change family relationships, but not the homosexuality itself. If only one parent is informed and the information is being kept from the other parent for one reason or another, it greatly increases the burden of tension between them. Without disclosure there can be no "talking it out" and no mutual support between the parents.

Perhaps other children in the family are aware of the sexual preference of their sibling and can interact with each other and with one or both parents in a way that can be mutually helpful. As I mentioned in chapter 1, a brother or sister is often the first to know.

The issues of what went wrong are best struggled with verbally and with someone who can really listen. If a spouse *will* not talk, it is desirable to seek out a good and trusted confidant: a friend, another family member, a minister. Disturbing thoughts get less disturbing when shared. If there is no one close to turn to, consider seeking help with a professional caregiver. Sessions during which thoughts and feelings can be expressed concerning possible errors in childrearing and exploring family relationships could relieve some pressure. Feelings about spouse and self can be explored. The process of restating your many thoughts and emotions out loud in the presence of an understanding other person is the beginning of working through this difficult phase of looking for what went wrong and finding some guidance on where to go from here.

Do not overlook the real possibility that help may be found by talking to your homosexual son or daughter. Most revelations of homosexuality are made by young people or adults who want to live honestly with themselves and their families. They have frequently gone through a process of struggling with a lot of emotional turmoil themselves before they tell their parents. It is likely that you can profitably share your misgivings with your child and get helpful feedback.

Bill reported on a conversation with his mother who had been widowed when Bill was seven and who had raised him alone on a small salary:

I've thought and thought about all this, Bill, and I just feel sure that if only I had let you play football when you were in high school, you wouldn't be like this. I remember well telling you on your first day at the high school that football scared me to death, and I said you just could not play. You didn't say a word, and I remember feeling uneasy, but glad that you hadn't argued. I wish I could do it all over again; I would certainly let you play any sport you wanted to. Bill smiled at his mother, and putting his hands on her shoulder, he replied: Mom, I remember that day too. I was so relieved to be *ordered* not to play football. I never wanted to. I was little, remember? And I wasn't very coordinated either. I was afraid they would make hamburger out of me if I ever got out on that field. You only beat me to the punch. I wanted to play in the band more than anything and I couldn't have done both.

After further discussion with her son this mother was able finally to rest in the knowledge that she hadn't been a perfect parent but that her son saw her as having done the best she could, which many times, was just right.

Self-blame and guilt are natural and quite common. With the self-searching, and especially in regard to other feelings, searching aloud with your spouse, other family members, friends, a minister, a professional counselor, you'll find that your unrealistic self-blame and guilt will gradually diminish to the vanishing point, and behavior that has stimulated appropriate guilt can be forgiven by a spouse, by the child, by God, and most important, by yourself.

6   If Our Child Only Loved Us . . .

Many parents at one time or another feel angry with their homosexual sons and daughters for their *being* homosexual or sometimes for *telling* them, the parents, about it. Some parents appear not to experience such anger, but many do. In chapter 2, I reported what one father's first direct verbal response was to his son after he found out: "It's a good thing you're not around here. I'd kill you." Another young man talked of his father's outbursts of rage in which the father called him all sorts of names. Some young people have been angrily banished from their homes: "You can come back when you've changed to how you're supposed to be!"

Anger is a natural human emotion when we are deeply hurt or frustrated or afraid. Anger toward someone else may also be anger that is felt toward oneself but is shifted to another target. Youth or young adults who are homosexual and who are telling or writing about their sexual orientation often begin by saying, "Now please don't be mad, but . . ." Of course, what they are expressing is their own discomfort with their parents' angry displeasure, but naturally they are making a request that is unreasonable for a large majority of parents. They *are* hurt, or frustrated, or afraid, or feel a combination of these emotions, and therefore they probably also are going to be angry. Although most of us parents have properly understood our task as assisting our children to move from independence to autonomy, giving them more and more freedom as they are ready for it, there are numerous times when children exercise their freedom in ways that don't meet our image, built up over the years, of who *our* child is going to be and how he or she is going to act. We are angry over our loss of control, even though in our better moments we have always known that we could not control them forever. We have just always dreamed that they would exercise control over their own lives in the ways that we would control them if we could. Oh, parenting! The joys and sorrows, the satisfactions and the pain, our own very real conflicts. This is just the way most of us are, so often experiencing our children's variance from us as if it were something done personally *against* us.

Now a son or daughter has told you that he or she is gay or lesbian. Gay? Lesbian? Most parents don't even like the words. Often enough one of the first reactions is, Why is our child doing this to us? It is not unusual for parents who are hit so hard by their shattered dreams, the sense of the loss of their son or daughter, the feeling of helplessness in a situation where control has slipped away from them, to shoot at targets wherever they can find them. They tell themselves it is someone else's fault, and they are angry with that person (chapter 4). It is their own fault as parents (chapter 5). It is the kids' fault. "They've always known what we've stood for. They've been raised in the church. They're bound to have assimilated the values we've held to be most important. Therefore, they know that this is wrong. They must be doing this to hurt us. If they only loved us, they wouldn't be this way."

For so many parents it comes as such a brutal shock. Your sons or daughters have been so "good" in so many ways. They may have been obedient. They have seemed to care about what you think. They have gone to Sunday school. You have certainly been led to believe that their value systems, their ideals, their faith in God was the same as, or at least similar to yours.

But homosexuality is such a *radical* difference. It feels like a stab in the back. "Have I been wrong about her all this time? How long has this hidden rebellion been going on? Can I trust him now when he says he truly loves me and doesn't want to hurt me? I'm not sure. Not now, anyway. I *do* hurt. She must have known how this would make me feel. If she *really* loved me, she wouldn't have *done* this to me."

Anger is understandable. But the anger is often accompanied by the kind of thinking just described. This type of thinking has two flaws. First, it assumes intentionality on the son's or daughter's part in *being* homosexual, and second, it assumes a single cause-effect system in human behavior. "If you really loved me, you wouldn't have *chosen* to feel, act, *be* this way. Your lack of love for me, your rebellion against me, has produced this behavior and in turn is proof that you don't love me." None of the elements of this circular argument holds up under the facts. As I shall explain in chapter 8, the human condition of being homosexual is not a condition that is chosen. Whatever is involved in a person's being gay or lesbian, the influences started at conception or very early in that person's life, or both, and developed over many years, covering the years of childhood dependence and then moving on into adolescence. Certain *acts,* indeed, are chosen, but the *condition* itself is *not* chosen in any simple and self-conscious way. In addition, human behavior is so complex that it rarely, if ever, is accurate to suggest a simple cause-effect product. It makes no more sense to say, "If he really loved me, he wouldn't be this way, or he would change," than it does to say, "If I'd only played ball more with my son," or "If I hadn't let her run around and play with those little boys all the time she wouldn't be this way." Such explanations of the human condition and human behavior are too simple, inadequate, and therefore *wrong.*

Anger is understandable. This sort of *thinking,* however, doesn't fit the facts. Now let's be thoroughly honest. There may be angry or rebellious elements in a son's or daughter's homosexual *behavior,* some of the ways in which it is acted out, or the setting or manner in which the child tells the parents about it. Many children of all ages, heterosexual and homosexual, do get angry with their parents, and their sexual acting out may be one way they express their feelings toward their parents. Husbands and wives occasionally do this to each other too, as a matter of fact. But your child's anger is not *the* reason he or she is gay or lesbian. The anger of your homosexual son or daughter toward you and now your anger toward your son or daughter needs to be traced to its roots and dealt with openly on that basis if you are to have a good relationship with each other. However, it is unrealistic for you to expect that when your child's anger diminishes and the rebellion vanishes, the child will automatically become heterosexual *because he or she now loves you.* (Even in the anger and rebellion, by the way, your son or daughter probably never *did* stop loving you.)

There is another difficulty in these early days following the discovery of a child's homosexuality. The "if he/she only loved me, he/she wouldn't be this way" as an expression of hurt and anger may all too easily be transformed into an attempt to create guilt in the child in order to manipulate him or her. Feeling that they are losing control over their child, some parents now try to regain it in this way.

A man in his late twenties was referred to me by a minister, who reported that according to the parents their son had been having some trouble with homosexual feelings and wanted help with this problem. Would I see him? Yes. He came in. Following my usual procedure for dealing with a referral, I began something like this: "You know that Reverend Johnson called and told me what your parents had told him. That puts me about three steps away from *you*, and yet *you're* the one who's here. I wonder if you'd be willing to tell me as honestly as you can your own real reasons for coming to see me."

The young man seemed to be surprised by this approach, because he first looked somewhat startled, then he hung his head, looked a bit sheepish, then looked back up and said, "Because my mother wanted me to." My next question was, "But what is it *you* want?" As it turned out, he had not simply been "bothered" recently by homosexual feelings. He had had them for about fifteen years and had finally come to the conclusion that he really was gay and that this was the way he wanted to be. He was in love with a man he had been living with for several months. He was well established in the homosexual and straight communities. He didn't desire to change his sexual orientation at all. But he also genuinely loved his parents. Their attitude had been that if he *really* cared for them and the rest of the family, he would get help to try to change. But he didn't *want* to change. A terrible conflict for him! He wanted to be as he *was*, but he also wanted to "prove" his love for his parents and his desire to please them. His fear was that if he didn't try to change, they would *never* be pleased with him. The alternative, which the young man expressed, was his desire that they love him as their son, as he was, and that he be allowed to be as much a part of the family as he had been when they didn't know about his being gay.

Most parents feel angry in the early days (weeks, sometimes months) after discovering that their son or daughter is gay or lesbian. This is understandable, and their children need to appreciate the fact that because of who their parents are, their anger is natural. But how are parents to express their anger?

If over the long haul you truly want to maintain a good relationship with your son or daughter, try to avoid these three responses. First, violence, name-calling, personal abuse, threats, banishment are *all* counterproductive. They express the anger, but they don't change your son's or daughter's homosexuality. They don't motivate him or her to change. They often drive a wedge more deeply between you.

Second, pretending that you are *not* angry doesn't work, because the anger continues to fester inside you, causing you more pain, and it inevitably comes out in disguised forms (against each other as parents, hurting behavior toward the child, depression). One mother in her rage frequently wrote vitriolic, accusatory, demeaning letters to her son. He finally responded by telling her clearly that they weren't going to get anywhere so long as she expressed herself that way to him. Then on her birthday he sent her a present. Her very next letter thanked him for remembering her, and the whole tone of this and the following letters was sweet, filled with news, just like the "old" times, as if nothing had happened. But something had happened, and it stretches the imagination too far to think that her feelings had changed so suddenly and radically. She had gotten the point that what she had been doing was destructive to the relationship, and she apparently really didn't want that. So she changed her behavior. But I believe that her anger was still there. She and her son both had to realize that if anger was there, it needed to be out in the open between them, although in a less negative form.

Third, given the opportunity to think through what we have been discussing in this chapter, we see that to express anger through the if-you-only-loved-me statement and our attempt to react to our helplessness in this new situation by using that approach may induce guilt in the child, and it just plain doesn't work.

If you are angry, just say so to your son or daughter. Try to be in touch with the intensity of the hurt, the shattered dreams, the frustration, the wanting it to be different but feeling helpless and afraid. These feelings should be shared between husband and wife and between parent and child. Remember, these feelings are the original sources of your anger, and when these other emotions and the experiences that produce them are fully felt and talked about and begin to diminish, the anger also will gradually diminish and usually disappear. Also be aware that a part of love is revealing ourselves even when we are afraid of the consequences, even when it will make us vulnerable, even when we are aware that there will be hurt involved. Sons and daughters are usually aware that this may happen when they reveal to their parent their homosexual orientation. When parents then also make themselves vulnerable to their sons and daughters as they speak of their own hurt and fear and disappointment, the anger toward one another in this situation loses much of its power.

7   What Will People Think?

"Hello, Ed. It's good to see you. How're your kids?"

"Just fine, Joe. How's your family?"

"Great. Joe, Jr. got married about six months ago, you know. We went up to Seattle for the wedding. It was a great time. Joe really got himself a fine girl. By the way, has old Bill gotten married yet?"

"No, not yet."

"Well, he had better hurry up. He's twenty-eight or twenty-nine now, isn't he?"

"Twenty-nine."

"Well, he's a nice-looking kid, and he's a fine person, too. You're lucky to have a son like that. Some girl will get him before long."

"Yeah."

"I've gotta be moving on. Good to see you, Ed. Tell your wife and kids hello for me."

"Yeah, nice to see you, too, Joe. Same to your family."

The men move away from each other on the street.

How it hurts! I don't want to see anyone I know. I can't look them in the eye. I feel so ashamed. They're bound to be able to read it in my face. So, little Joe got married. I remember getting the invitation now. I felt real pleased then. Thought there was still hope for Bill. That was just about a month before he told us. *My* son! In love with another man! Been living with him for a year. We knew he had a roommate. But they're *lovers*! Why do people have to ask about him? Why do they want to know if he's married yet? I lie through my teeth! There's no *way* I can tell them the truth! What would they think about us? about Bill? How could I call on customers and expect to get any kind of reception? We'd never be able to hold our heads up in public anymore. We've practically stopped going to church the last few weeks. I feel so out of place there now. If they only knew! They couldn't understand. I already feel as if everybody's eyes are glued on me when I walk in anyway. I just can't take it. Somehow it all feels so dirty. It's like *I'd* done something.

"Has old Bill gotten married yet? He'd better hurry up." A parent *feels* the unspoken message: There's something wrong with him. There's something wrong with you. There's a feeling of shame that somehow you've betrayed your family, your church, the human race. You just can't shake it.

Somehow this feels different from guilt. Guilt is our awareness that we *have* done something wrong that we have actually been responsible for. We have violated a standard, broken a rule or a law. Whether anyone else knows it or not, we know it within ourselves. Shame is the feeling that we have in the face of our failure to live up to an ideal, and somehow it has something to do with the way other people would think and feel about us if they knew about it. Guilt is internalized: *I* see it as wrong regardless of what other people think. Shame is what I feel when other people recognize or see that I don't live up to the community ideal.

In regard to your son's or daughter's being homosexual, Ed's feelings are somewhat realistic. He and his wife and other members of his family share the same unspoken yet unquestioned expectations that a large percentage of society has: Children will grow up heterosexual, they will probably marry (and are deviant and somewhat suspect if they don't), and they will probably have children. This pattern is a social ideal that most of us have unconsciously adopted as our own, as unfair as it actually is to a lot of people when we stop to think about it. Nevertheless, the failure to *achieve* this ideal is part of the homosexual person's own grappling with her or his identity and the feeling of shame, feeling very bad about one's self, and having the very low self-esteem that is often a characteristic part of their reactions to the growing awareness of their sexual orientation, at least during the early stages and, for some, for a much longer time. Being linked together as we are in families, and due to a natural tendency to see families as a single entity within which differences are not expected, other persons within the family feel shame also. Therefore, homosexuality, like a variety of other "family failures" (alcoholism and mental illness, for example), must be kept secret. Other people must never know, you think, or we'll all be social outcasts. What will people think about us? They will probably think about us as we are now thinking and feeling about ourselves—shame, that we are bad parents, that something mysterious and wrong has been going on in our house.

A young man reported his observations of his parents' reactions. The father in particular had a sense of near desperation about the possibility that someone in the town would find out. He repeatedly told his wife: "Don't dare tell anyone. If anyone finds out about this, I'm going to have to leave. I just can't face people if they know this." With these words, he was expressing the depth of his shame, the intensity of his own terrible feelings, the social fear. But he was also stating it in such a way that it came across as a threat to his wife. "If you tell, I'll have to leave you." And so this threat became a barrier between them at a time when they needed each other more than ever. The mother wanted to try to work it all through with her son as quickly as possible so she could truly accept him in an easy relationship once again. But the father was saying, "The more you try to understand, the worse you make it for me." His reaction placed his wife in a position of great conflict; even in her hurt and disappointment she felt an urge to understand and accept her own son, but she was being told that to do so would be to push her husband away from her. What a tragically difficult situation!

It is not unusual for parents to agree with each other that they will tell no one else. So at a time when they desperately need the love (if not total understanding) and the support of other family members, of friends and neighbors and fellow workers, of the church, they keep it a secret. To do this only intensifies the feelings of isolation they already have. The parents whose reactions I have just described told me this: "There's literally *no one* we can talk to about this. We don't know a single family in this town who's experienced this. There's no one."

People feel they must keep shame to themselves, and yet the sense of isolation that is intensified by keeping the secret also further feeds the feelings of shame. It is a destructive trap. Isolation also leads to a breakdown of reality-testing, that normal sharing of things we have heard, of our perceptions and interpretations of all sorts of things, as part of everyday conversation. As we express these, some perceptions are confirmed, but we also hear conflicting information and receive different perceptions and interpretations. This constant testing and retesting of our sense of things is necessary to keep our thinking clear and reasonably accurate and thus to reduce feelings of suspicion, fear, threat, and inappropriate anger that otherwise would have free rein and make our lives unhappy and ineffective.

I have already indicated the importance of parents' talking with each other, with other members of the family, with selected good and trusted friends, or perhaps with their minister or a professional counselor. How blessed also are those parents who have within their local church congregation a prayer group, a Sunday school class, or a small sharing group where they can tell the others that their child is homosexual. Lacking this, look for some organization that offers support groups for family members of gays and lesbians. You'll quickly discover that there *are* numerous other families who have similar experiences. You can express to these concerned persons what you yourselves are experiencing and receive from this group love and understanding and continued support.

When the parents of the young man mentioned above told him that they didn't know any family who had had this experience, he immediately told them of several within their circle of friends and acquaintances. They were not as alone as they thought.

When some parents begin with dread to tell their other children that their brother or sister is homosexual, it is not uncommon for these other children to respond, "Oh, I've thought (or "known") that for a long time."

Of course, you cannot avoid social reality. Some people *won't* understand. Some people *may* pull away from you. Some minister *may* be condemnatory. Some customer may *not* buy from you anymore. None of us has control over the thoughts, feelings, or behavior of other people. They will say what they'll say, just as they do in other situations. To this extent, there is some risk for you. But there is a *much greater risk* in allowing your desire to keep it all hidden to dictate your behavior to the point that you hide and lie and pretend. This type of behavior is usually very damaging to persons and relationships.

Therefore, to whom shall we tell what? With some exceptions, it is important to inform fully both parents and every member of the immediate family and other members of the family whom you would expect to see. As I indicated in chapter 1, it is fairly common for a homosexual young person or young adult to tell a brother or a sister first and then tell one or both parents. It is also more frequent, judging from my experience, for the child to tell the mother first rather than the father or the two of them together, or merely to tell the mother but not the father. This observation of mine is at least in line with, although not proved by, Bell and Weinberg's study of homosexual persons themselves. Forty percent of the white males reported that they thought their mothers definitely knew about their sexual orientation, while only 33 percent thought their fathers knew. Nearly 50 percent of the white females thought their mothers definitely knew, and 40 percent thought their fathers knew. This is not the same as their having specifically *told* their mothers and/or fathers, and, of course, some of them may *not* have told and are guessing wrong about their parents' knowledge. But it is interesting that with both male and female, it is the mothers who are pointed to more often as knowing, and it is the mothers in my experience who time and again are pointed to by their children as probably being more understanding and willing to work through their feelings and the issues openly. It does not always turn out that way, but more often than not it does.[1]

However, *both* parents need to know. If a mother says, "We mustn't tell your father; I don't know what he'd do," or if a father says, "We can't tell your mother; it'll just kill her," you need to take a hard look at what that may mean. First, this type of response on the part of a parent may reflect that something is already quite wrong with the relationship between the husband and wife. Second, it may create (or strengthen) a divisive coalition in the family, pitting one parent and the child against the other parent. This speaks to the inadequacy of the ways in which husband and wife meet each other's needs. Finally, trying to keep the secret from one parent causes additional stress within the family, as does any pattern of covering up and withholding. A parent may think that he or she is protecting the spouse and therefore is doing something good for the other. But this is no protection. It is usually better to get the truth out, then deal together with the feelings and issues as they are shared openly with one another. Whatever else, this is the child of *both* parents. When there is a stepparent, that person needs to know, as well as does the corresponding original parent.

Brothers and sisters need to be told, and most properly by the homosexual person, although it may be that the parents would be present for that session. The parents' presence may be especially important if the siblings being told are in their mid-teens or younger. The homosexual son or daughter may, of course, want to tell older brothers and sisters without the parents being present. I believe that they have this right, although everyone would not agree. Brothers and sisters will find out or be told eventually, so it's better that they be told now in a straightforward way at their particular level of understanding. It is true, of course, that sometimes brothers and sisters who are adults move away from each other, have little communication, sometimes have intense conflict, and that in some circumstances a responsible choice is made not to inform them, but this is rare.

The same is true of grandparents, aunts, uncles, and cousins who are close, not only geographically but also in terms of genuine caring. How do you go about it?

We have something that we have to tell you because we know that you love us and Marie. She has just told us she is lesbian. We're deeply disappointed and hurt and confused and angry. We feel bad about ourselves and are feeling guilty. But we love her and are trying to understand and work this through with each other. We need your support and prayers in this effort. Marie, of course, was anxious about telling us and is anxious about your knowing, but she also believed that it was important to our family life to be open and honest. She loves you, and although it may be difficult, wants to be able to talk with you about it the next time you see each other.

Naturally, you would use words that genuinely fit your experience and are applicable to your son or daughter. It may also be that in your situation it is more appropriate that your son or daughter write or talk to the relatives than for you to do so.

There will, of course, likely be some exceptions to what I have been recommending here. Each homosexual person, along with the parents, will need to talk the matter over in detail and weigh the advantages and disadvantages of communicating all this to the family.

Depending on circumstances, you may feel it is important to tell some close friends, neighbors, the minister, or people at the church, as you feel the need and as the occasion arises. The point to grow toward, and it certainly takes growth for quite a majority, is to be able to respond spontaneously in the middle of a conversation. When Joe says, "By the way, has old Bill gotten married yet?" you'll be able to reply, "No, Joe, he hasn't and he won't. Bill told us a few months ago that he was gay. It was a real blow to us, and it left our heads spinning. We had to go through a lot with each other, but we're working it out. And that's just the way it is." Again, obviously, you would use words to describe yourself as you actually are in this situation.

Once again, I want to remind you that you are not alone, and it is both unrealistic and hurtful to think and act as if you were. Every homosexual person has parents, and they live around you, and some of them may already be your friends. If some of you could identify one another, it would be natural and productive for you to share your experiences and band together in getting information that will guide your thinking and your feeling reactions. This could be done through informal conversations and with just a bit of planning effort. In addition, if there is no chapter of Parents, Family and Friends of Lesbians and Gays in your area, perhaps you and some other couples might explore the possibility of starting a larger group that would meet regularly to discuss related problems and gain information. Your group may grow large enough to become an affiliate (see Additional Resources under Support Groups).

Within your church, you will probably encounter persons who understand and persons who don't. Some will actively seek to support you, and others, in reacting to their own feelings of intense discomfort, will pull away. Likewise, some ministers can be extremely helpful to you, while others will not be able to help at all. There are only two alternatives. One is to keep silent and thereby fail to receive the personal sustenance you need. The other is to share the information and your experiences with fellow church members when it is appropriate to do so, realizing that some will be disconcerted and not know how to respond. Remember, that only by sharing will you be in a position to receive the helpful listening and expressions of love that you need from a number of others.

It is gratifying to know that an increasing number of congregations are discussing their responsibility for ministry to lesbians and gays and their families. A few have actually made a public declaration of their desire to be open to gays and lesbians in their worship, church school classes—in short, in the whole life of the church. Others, while not committing openly as a unified congregation, have a number of gay and lesbian members whose sexual orientation is known to many and who are well accepted. Few congregations as a whole are unanimous on anything, but it is a rare congregation that does not have compassionate people who will respond to your needs with support. You, however, will need to seek them out.

Finally, you are never "alone in the universe." In the midst of what is so often experienced as a terrible aloneness, feeling cut off from others whom until now you have thought you could count on, you may also feel deserted by God. If this is the case, even in this you are not alone. Jesus, and the psalmist before him (Ps. 22), cried out, "My God, my God, why hast thou forsaken me?" But the Bible makes clear that even though this is the way they *felt* at the time, God was still present with them and for them. God can assist you, too, in sustaining you as persons and as a family in the larger community in which you live as you struggle with your own feelings, your thoughts, and your relationships with one another.

8   What Causes Homosexuality, Anyway?

From what we have been saying up to this point, it should be clear that people's reactions to lesbians and gays and their attitudes about homosexuality seem to reflect a confusing vacillation between two strong emotional opinions. Somehow at one and the same time homosexuality is perceived as a dread personal and social disease that produces a sense of shame in the parents and that needs psychological treatment, but it is also willfully and perversely chosen immorality that the person could stop if only he or she wanted to, really loved the parents, accepted Christ, or whatever.

What is the source of this condition? Parents who are struggling with their own emotional reactions and their lack of understanding need help in trying to answer these questions for themselves in order to gain a more meaningful perspective. Unfortunately, while the discussion presented in this chapter may assist parents in understanding their homosexual son or daughter better, it is not likely to clear up all the confusion.

A great deal has been written and spoken about the subject for several decades. A clear definition of the word *homosexual* that is acceptable to all has not been found and may not be. For the purposes of this book, however, homosexuality is defined as a sexual attraction, emotional attachment, and/or sexual relations with someone of the same sex *over a substantial period of time in adult life.* (See the discussion of a definition in chapter 3.) This definition does not preclude sexual acts or emotional attachments or even marriage to a person of the other sex. Neither does it preclude a decision to remain celibate.

What is the cause (or the causes) of homosexuality? This is where the discussion really gets complicated. I will be as simple and clear as possible. There are still a few people around who believe that they know *the* cause, but the overwhelming majority of genuine experts, researchers using scientific methodology, are not at all sure that there is any one source of homosexuality. I shall review the two major theories briefly. The first has to do with developmental issues in the context of the family system of origin, and the second with genetics and physiology.

Over several decades numerous psychotherapists, each of whom has worked with a number of homosexual persons (far more gay men than lesbians), note that they have begun to see a particular family pattern of behavior that existed during the time the gay men in therapy were growing up. The trouble is, the descriptions of this pattern differ from one therapist to another. As many as nine different ones can be identified. A number of comments and criticisms must be made about this phenomenon.

First, there is no reason to doubt the integrity of the therapists. They undoubtedly discovered what they said they discovered. However, the source of their information was typically an adult who was sufficiently distressed as to seek professional help, and who in this distress was attempting to describe his or her mother and father and events in the home from an adult perspective many years later. Surely the picture verbally painted could not be expected to produce an exact portrayal of the character and behavior of the father and the mother or of their relationship with each other and with their child.

Second, as one reads the description of the family pattern that each therapist presents, it seems reasonable that some potential for its exerting a noxious influence upon the child did exist. But if a family pattern is to blame, why is it that other children in the families involved remained predominantly heterosexual? And why is it that each therapist consistently finds patterns that differ from those of all the other therapists? Of course, many of the parental characteristics portrayed in these theories do have areas of similarity, but they also vary sufficiently as to raise serious doubt about the validity of any one of them being *the* cause of homosexuality. Irving Bieber's statement, for example, "a constructive, supportive, warmly related father precludes the possibility of a homosexual son," is simply not true.[1] Another problem with the family pattern theory is apparent. Clinicians work also with men and women who, although their parents are "classical" homosexual producers, have remained definitely heterosexual.

Conversely, many gays and lesbians report not only adequate, but warm, loving, and well-functioning families. These tend to be persons who do not need to seek professional help. The trouble and pain experienced by homosexual persons (and heterosexual persons too) whose family experiences were less than ideal are the real forces that lead them into treatment. Being gay or lesbian is often the least of their problems.

If your son or daughter has taken the initiative to tell you about his or her sexual orientation, it may be encouraging for you to note that the homosexual person who wants to reveal this to the parents is exhibiting some faith in you and in the family system. Whether that faith has any basis in reality is tested in the ensuing process after the revelation.

If you are already feeling guilty about the possibility that you had a role in your son's or daughter's becoming homosexual, your feelings probably haven't been helped by any reading you have done about the mother's and father's responsibility for this. On the one hand, you may reject the implication that you are one of these "bad" families or persons. On the other hand, you may be blaming yourself and/or your spouse even more, because you can think of this or that thing you have done "wrong" (see chapter 5). Let me clarify this. I have been briefly describing families as they have been observed by psychotherapists or as they were perceived by the homosexual persons themselves who grew up in them. Even good, loving people have a variety of personal needs that lead them to relate in certain ways within their families, and these relationships affect us all within the family in complex ways; not all of these ways are positive. To interact with one another in a family in these complex and sometimes negative ways, and to have someone in the family be homosexual, alcoholic, or mentally ill is not the same thing as stating that one parent or both parents have *caused* the condition. Human behavior is so complex that there cannot be a simple, direct causation. Other factors also have a role. However, the way in which we seek to get our needs met by others within the family and the degree to which we do and do not meet one another's needs does have an influence on our emotional life and our behavior, including our "outside the family" behavior.

As a child develops from infancy into adulthood, a multitude of events, both external and internal, physiological and psychological, produce a particular and unique self. Each child is born into a particular family, to a particular mother who is in a particular stage of her own adolescent or adult development, fathered by a male parent in his particular stage. The child is born with his or her own pattern of genes that includes such critical items as sex, body shape and size, and neurological composition, especially those neural connections in the brain that control sexual function and those that will shape and/or limit our perception of the external world. This child is also born into a larger context of community and world in which specific conditions exist and specific events take place that can and do have a critical impact on parents and therefore on the child as well. As the child grows, she or he begins to make observations and come to conclusions about himself or herself and the world. The basic task for each child is to survive and then to feel comfortable and safe, to grow and begin to be a separate person capable of caring for oneself and for others. As each child goes through this process, he or she reaches conclusions that come to be perceived as the hard-and-fast rules of life. Sometimes the child develops rules that are distortions of reality as it now exists, but which he or she believed were essential at the time they were made.

Children go through specific and identifiable stages while growing up. Theorists use varying terms to identify these different stages, but all theorists agree there is nothing random about the progression from one developmental stage to the next. Sometimes because of a traumatic incident or because of a poorly functioning family system, a child may not go through a developmental stage successfully or completely. This child keeps right on growing and going through the rest of the stages, but the omission of this stage creates a distortion that remains to be corrected.

Throughout the stages of development the child is discovering and making decisions about his or her body, including factors that influence identity, how one views oneself as male or female, and how one relates to the same and to the other sex. These stages always derive from a compound of internal and external stimuli. The child arrives at puberty with this sexual identity now being compounded by the hormonal storms of adolescence. Clear and strong sexual feelings arise. Body size and contours change rapidly during these adolescent years. Many professionals in the field of human development would put the age of clear sexual identity much earlier than adolescence, although there is no agreement as to which age or in which stage of development it occurs.

In years past there have been those who explained the development of homosexuality in terms of learning theory. One learns to enjoy and repeat homosexual behavior, or one learns to enjoy and repeat heterosexual behavior, or both. In a sense we "learn" all our behavior, but this view is more complicated than it appears on the surface. Predisposition, or tendency to choose in one direction or the other, plays its role in who learns what and how well. But once a stimulus is experienced positively and is frequently repeated with the same results, it becomes "learned."

This sounded like good news for those who desired change from homosexuality to heterosexuality. If a person learns it, then it is possible to unlearn it and learn something else. A variety of behavioral therapies were used, usually without thorough change or lasting success. Behavior *is* learned, and behavior *can* be changed; but genetic/physiological predispositions cannot be changed, and very early childhood learning does not seem to be amenable to behavior therapy methods.

In general, principles of learning are valid, although various ones differ from one another. However, no single theory or combination of theories seems to account for the development of human personality unless they are combined with findings from a number of other sources. The methods of behavior therapy, based on the learning theories of the time, have not been sufficiently effective to substantiate the idea that homosexual orientation is learned.

The conclusion? I, along with many others, do not *know* with any high degree of certainty what *causes* homosexuality. That doesn't seem to be too helpful, does it? Consider in summary the potentials and limitations of genetic/physiological givens, the complexity and power of a family system, the influence of trauma and other powerful experiences upon a child's uneven movement through the developmental stages, the circumstances that lead a child to adopt a particular set of influential friends over others, and the variety of opportunities for learning about sex and what it means to be a boy or girl and potentially a man or woman. Think of the role of *all* this in developing one's self-image. It's difficult to imagine that where and with what group of people and how a child moves from infancy to adolescence and adulthood doesn't have something to do with the direction of one's primary sexual desires. Note that I have not said "causes," but has "something to do with." Remember that all infants do not come into the world exactly the same. Children go through the development summarized in general in the previous paragraph with a different genetic inheritance and other sources of physiological differences.

The first edition of this book was published at a time when I was more skeptical than I am now of the strength of the theory that genetic/neurological/hormonal sources may exist for homosexual orientation. More sophisticated research has been going on in recent years and continues at this time. The most suggestive of these are in three areas. The first comprises a group of studies that have examined at least two areas of the brain with the discovery that the size of each differed significantly between the homosexual men and the heterosexual men studied. Much remains to be known. These studies have not shown conclusively that *all* gay men exhibit such differences. But these are interesting beginnings that will undoubtedly produce more conclusive data in the future.

Even more significant in my thinking is a study in which the researchers have actually identified a DNA marker on the X-chromosome that distinguishes between a majority of the gay men studied and a heterosexual male control group. A number of twin studies also lead in the direction of strong genetic influence.

The third group of studies, covering a longer period of time than the others, has examined hormonal changes that occur in the mother during pregnancy. At least four sources of these changes have been isolated. Numerous researchers are convinced that these hormonal changes predispose the child to develop in the direction of gay or lesbian orientation.

And what about lesbians? The studies just mentioned have dealt primarily with men. Similar data at this time have not been collected for women. In fact, some authorities believe that the determining factors in the origin of sexual orientation for gays and lesbians may (or probably do) differ from each other. Do these studies *prove* that homosexuality is inherited, that it *is* a physiological condition? No. But together they are strongly suggestive of a genetic/physiological involvement. Most scientists themselves are very cautious about attributing a single cause to something as complex as human behavior. For example, body size in general is inherited, but the genes don't determine what we do with our sizes. Even size is affected by other factors (nutrition, exercise). At this point in time we can be open to the probability of genetic physiological factors, probably in complex interaction with family system and a number of other variables, that function to establish sexual orientation very early in one's life. The combination of variables, of course, differs from person to person.

What is very clear now is that being gay or lesbian is not a conscious choice that a person makes. We do not remain sexually neutral until our teen years or adulthood and then just decide, "I think I'll be heterosexual," or "I'll be homosexual." Neither do we approach puberty with either a heterosexual or a homosexual identity and then one day merely decide, "I just think I'll change."

Having said this, we have to allow for occasional exceptions. There are a few who do report having decided to be gay or lesbian. The chances are small that your child is among these, but if she or he states that it was a choice, this opens up a new area of conversation for you.

Many gay and lesbian people have themselves grown up with the customary family and social expectations: having friends of the other sex, dating persons of the other sex, even marrying, believing that they are heterosexual (or trying to be), but gradually becoming more and more aware that this is not working, that something is "wrong" with the way they are living. As they gradually become aware that they have been conforming to a social norm that doesn't include who they really are, the only choice left to them is whether to acknowledge to themselves, to admit, "I'm gay," "I'm lesbian."

Many also state that from the time of their first memories they knew they were different. They didn't know what that meant in terms of adult sexuality, of course, but they felt different from their same-sex playmates. Once sexual feelings began to flourish at puberty, however, they began to see more clearly how they were different; they had sexual feelings for persons of the same sex. Though this is not conclusive proof that they "were born that way," it may reflect some of the physiological differences described above. These physiological factors may also have functioned in interaction with a variety of early influences that at this time they cannot clearly identify, but which may be discovered by some individuals, usually during the process of psychotherapy.

Some of the practical implications of this discussion on physiological factors may be that it will mitigate parents' blaming themselves or one another or perhaps help to change some family members' belief that being homosexual is a perverse choice on the part of a son or daughter and that the person *could* change if she or he only would. Blame is not appropriate or helpful.

Another practical implication of the best information we now have regarding the possible sources of homosexual orientation, together with the experience of untold numbers of gays and lesbians, is that even when they have *wanted* to change, wanted for whatever reason or combination of reasons to become genuinely heterosexual, they were unable to do so. They went to psychiatrists or clergy; they prayed and sought God's help. But it was for naught, and it brought them only more frustration and agony.

Most parents have wanted desperately for their children to change, and parents are not to be faulted for that. But the efforts of the child of whatever age to do what their parents want, to please or placate or to avoid the penalties of any threats that are made, have been even more unsuccessful and frustrating. To be sure, for more than thirty years a few psychotherapists from time to time have claimed to have succeeded in facilitating the change from homosexuality to heterosexuality in a fairly large percentage of their "patients." From the late 1950s I read several books by these therapists with great interest and rising optimism. I haven't been aware of new claims of such success since about 1980, and my own experience in assisting gay men who desired such change to accomplish it—either through my own efforts or by referring them to psychiatrists—has been dismal. What initially looked like progress for as long as four years was later reported to me by some of these gay men as self-delusion, supported by me and other professionals. They were definitely gay.

You may also have read or heard about claims by some Christian groups or individuals that through the power of God and the support of a Christian community, homosexual feelings in certain people have been taken away, enabling them to live as heterosexuals. If this has been the experience of a former gay or lesbian person, I have no grounds for saying that this is not so. In some thirty-five years of pastoral counseling with gays and lesbians, however, many of whom I am certain really wanted to change, had sincere and strong motivation to change, and were committed Christians, I have not known even one who was able to do so. Some were and still are conservative evangelical Christians.

I can only conclude at this point in time that if a lesbian or gay person definitely wants to change, especially if he or she is a teenager or a very young adult, it could be important to tell the person of your support of his or her exploring whether this is possible with the help of a competent and compassionate psychiatrist who has experience working with gays and lesbians. Likewise, it is important to encourage the person to pray and engage in other spiritual disciplines and to consult with a spiritual director. It is crucial that the person have the guidance of a spiritually sensitive and experienced person, since there are so many counterproductive ways to pray. The goal is increased openness to God. Some may discover that their gay feelings and experiences have grown out of unique circumstances and needs, and in so doing, they may rediscover their suppressed or repressed heterosexuality. Even if they do not change, however, the professional guidance and/or their spiritual disciplines and deepened faith will have helped them in other ways; it may also help them not to blame themselves for "failing." They have not, nor have you.

Parents will need to reassure children throughout the process and at its conclusion that they love and support them *just as they are.* For parents to attempt to force change by threats of any kind, by psychological pressure, by withholding love, by ostracism, by banishment, or other means will produce not a change in sexual orientation, but anger and alienation.

Genuine homosexual orientation might well be rooted, to some extent, in hereditary factors and perhaps other physiological conditions. If family system influences and/or the impact of trauma are also factors, their occurence in life would have been before the person's conscious decision-making took place. Because of this, whatever combination of forces may have contributed, to change who they are sexually will be highly improbable if not impossible. This is the reality that gays and lesbians themselves and their families must ultimately accept.

The mystery of exactly why and how homosexual orientation comes about will likely remain uncertain for some time, but by removing the stigma and hatred and by gaining insights from continued research, we can move forward to acceptance and reconciliation within the families of lesbians and gays.

9 But Doesn't the Bible Condemn It?

For parents who are Christians, who belong to the church, and who find real meaning in participation in the church, the question posed in this chapter title is pertinent. Although we parents are quite probably aware of our own sins and shortcomings, to the extent that we are deeply serious about our Christian commitment, these sins are painful to us. Our response when we sin is properly to seek forgiveness and renewal of life in the Spirit and then move on. But homosexuality! It really seems so different to us. It *feels* different when it is our own son or daughter who is involved, and regardless of what we say or do, he or she doesn't seem to change and perhaps doesn't even want to. It is as if this child, who has been so dear to us, now continues to live a life that we understand the Bible and Christian tradition to condemn. A man I know literally groans with agony when he speaks of his son's living in sin and his seeming unwillingness to make a conscientious attempt to change. This is a deeply emotional issue for many parents, and I want to deal with it at that level of seriousness.

There is little question that the mainstream of Christian tradition over the centuries has been such as to make homosexuals feel either unwelcome or uncomfortable, or both, in the church. Only in recent years have any Christian groups ordained into their ministry persons who were openly known as homosexual. With the exception of the Metropolitan Community Church, which is a growing association of congregations whose ministry is primarily directed to gays, such ordinations are still quite rare. Many people, though, are aware that there are gays and lesbians in the ministry of the mainline churches and that there always have been. They simply are not usually *known* to be gay. The ministry of these hidden homosexuals has been pretty much like that of heterosexuals: effective, ineffective, or somewhere in between, depending on the gifts and graces and willingness to work that they bring to it, not on their sexual orientation. I have personally known numerous gays and lesbians in ministry and have corresponded with others. They have been in several different denominations, including very conservative ones. Some of them are pastors of large churches and are well respected.

Presumably this tradition against the inclusion of known homosexuals in the life of the community of faith has been based upon what seem to be anti-homosexual passages in the Bible. Some parents who are in the church (or even who have been in the past) use the Bible as a way of expressing their horror at and anger against their children. One mother almost immediately responded to her son when he told her that he was gay with these words: "Haven't you read your Bible? Don't you know what it says?" However, what struck the son most about her reaction was that she had never taken the Bible that seriously before. Some parents insist that their children read the passages condemning homosexuality, as if somehow it would motivate them to change. It doesn't. Even when the lesbian or gay is a sincere Christian, by the time the person tells the parents of her or his sexual orientation, he or she often has already dealt with the biblical issue, the sin issue.

Since the Bible is certainly clear enough that heterosexuals can sin (and most of us have accumulated sufficient personal evidence to support that fact), then homosexuality must somehow have been viewed (and continues to be viewed) by a large number of Christians as being a different order of sin. How could this be so? It seems to me that there is a great deal of confusion at this point. The Bible is not ambiguous on one issue: "All have sinned and fall short of the glory of God" (Rom. 3:23), and "There is no one who is righteous, not even one" (3:10). The Bible does not designate different orders of sin, except perhaps in the difficult reference by Jesus to an "unpardonable sin," but by no stretch of the imagination can we infer from that text that he is speaking of homosexuality (Matt. 12:31–32; Mark 3:28–30; Luke 12:10; almost identical wording). As a matter of fact, Jesus never refers to homosexuality at all. Therefore, homosexuality must be like other sin and yet *not* like other sin at the same time. Again, how can this be? I propose two responses: One is on an emotional level and the other on the level of how we go about trying to understand the scripture.

First, let me ask you a question. Do you take *all* biblical injunctions with equal seriousness and emotional intensity? Just think about it a minute before you read further. For example, are you part of a crusade to stop the crossbreeding of cattle or the planting of more than one crop in a single field? Do you refuse to wear clothing that is made of more than one kind of fiber? Ridiculous questions! Yet these are definitely prohibited in Leviticus 19:19, which is part of the same Holiness Code that was compiled from several earlier sources and reached its present form in the sixth century B.C. It also states, "You shall not lie with a male as with a woman" (18:22), which apparently was written *to men only*, the same prohibition being also repeated in 20:13.

Do you take all biblical injunctions with the same seriousness? Obviously not! Do you understand all the statements of this *whole* code (Leviticus 17 to 26) to be equally applicable centuries later? Read all ten chapters, seriously, not only with reference to the several different things we have already mentioned but also with its guidelines for making burnt sacrifices, harvesting crops, how priests should dress and do their hair, and so forth. Obviously, none of us follows all of this to the letter. Do you even want to apply literally the two verses dealing with homosexuality? Probably not. In addition to the point already made, that it is apparently *written* only to men, both verses *apply* literally only to males. They do not explicitly prohibit sexual relations between women. (Does that now immediately change the way you feel about your *daughter's* situation?) The other fact is that Leviticus 20:13 requires the death penalty for a male homosexual act. Even to the extent that your own feelings toward a son who is homosexual may be extremely negative, do you believe that it justifies the death penalty?

Literally hundreds of illustrations may exist that would indicate that *none* of us interprets all biblical commandments as having the same degree of relevance for our lives today; nor do we have the same intensity of emotional reaction to all commandments. Why is this true? First, we have different sets of experiences that lead us into radically different emotional responses to different behaviors. (For example, our experience with wearing cloth made of two fibers has usually been that it is really not such a big deal. We have never been threatened by it; it is not socially disruptive or personally harmful.) Second, a basic principle of biblical interpretation tells us that some biblical statements do not apply to us *today* in *our* society as they did to the people of *that* day in *their* society, while other biblical statements not only are still relevant but are authoritative as well. How do you do that? On what basis do you accept some and reject others?

In all honesty, it has been my experience that in the church our emotional reaction against homosexuality is not prompted by the fact that the *Bible* condemns it, but that *we* as human beings condemn it. Even if we knew nothing at all about the Bible, we would condemn it. We condemn it because of what we have learned from our society, because of our misconceptions about persons who are homosexual, about who they are and what they do, and because from time to time either it has touched our lives or we have heard of it when it has touched the lives of others in ways that arouse our fear, revulsion, and anger. This is not to suggest that if people only had accurate information they would inevitably think that homosexuality was perfectly all right; I am simply stating the conviction that the intensity of emotional reaction against homosexuality comes from a variety of social learning factors and from personal experiences rather than from the interpretation that the Bible says that it is wrong.

Read 1 Corinthians 6:9 and 1 Timothy 1:10. Do you experience the same negative emotional response to the greedy, idolaters, liars, slanderers, and perjurers as you do to homosexual behavior? Probably not. Ask yourself honestly, "Why not?" The New Testament makes no distinction between the seriousness of these sins.

Most of us are familar with cases in which men have been sentenced to prison because they have fondled young boys and exposed themselves to them. Often the public reaction is to label that behavior as homosexuality: "That's what we have to fear!" Certainly there is something to fear when this type of incident takes place, but these men are rarely homosexual. They suffer from pedophilia, a serious psychological disorder. Or we may read of a homosexual affair that ends in a jealous fight and murder. Of course that happens, but far less often than it does in heterosexual quarrels, which also end in violence and death. Just note the prevalence of spousal (usually husband on wife) abuse.

We feel revulsion, fear, and anger in response to homosexuality. Then we *use* the Bible (or at least what we have *heard* about the Bible) to support *our* emotional reactions. As Christians, we are not free to condone any sin, but do we respond to all sin, or *all* sinners, with the same emotional intensity we reserve for homosexuality? Most of us just do not. For example, how do we perceive white-collar crime (jockeying figures on books to someone's financial advantage)? And what about blue-collar crime (just a few boards and pieces of pipe and a tool or two from the plant. Sure, it says "Thou shalt not steal," but the company is so big, so rich, they'll never miss it)? Do we also get enraged about what the Bible points to as the *central* sin, idolatry, the sin from which all others come, having some other god before Jehovah God? Let's isolate socially all people who bear false witness. Let's root them out of the church. Let's condemn vigorously all who do not keep the sabbath (literally, Friday sundown to Saturday sundown). Let's not ordain anyone who covets. "*All* have sinned and fall short of the glory of God," and the sin of many of us sinners is to view other sinners as far worse sinners than we, and so we condemn *them* and place restrictions on *them* in the church.

We have to deal with the Leviticus verses, of course. They command that the male homosexual act not take place. (Also notice that they do not command a man not to *be* homosexual or to have homosexual *feelings*.) It is an *act* that these verses condemn. If, on the basis that the purpose of the entire Holiness Code is to clarify and maintain the distinctive integrity of the Hebrew people as the people of God in contrast with the other nations around them, we make a judgment that the injunctions found in the Code are thus not necessarily applicable to many other people, Christian people, in different nations of the world today, then why do we pay attention to some of these commandments but ignore others? One way many Christians would respond to this is by suggesting that we test the older Jewish practices by New Testament standards and guidelines, the revelation of God in *Christ*. If this is one of our principles of biblical interpretation, then at least temporarily we must set aside the Leviticus verses until we look at the New Testament; therefore these two Leviticus verses cannot stand *by themselves* as being valid as a contemporary commandment any more than the one that states, "If it [the peace offering sacrifice] is eaten at all on the third day, it is an abomination" (Lev. 19:7).

Before we go to the New Testament, however, we must take a trip to Sodom, since the events of one evening in that city have frequently been cited as presenting a condemnation of homosexuality. However, if a person reads the story carefully and also reads later references to Sodom in other books of the Bible, one will see that homosexuality *as such* is not the main focus of attention in the description of the city as being so sinful that it should be destroyed. (There is a somewhat similar story in Judges 19, but not located in Sodom.) A brief summary here will suffice. For those who desire to read in greater detail about Sodom or the whole issue of the Bible's dealing with homosexuality, we suggest that you read chapters in three other books, although they differ somewhat from one another in certain details of interpretation. (See entries under "Homosexuality, the Bible, and the Church" in Additional Resources.)

In the first place, it is quite clear in the Genesis 19 story that the men of the city wanted to have sexual relationships with Lot's two guests, who were actually angels disguised as men. However, it was not merely that they *wanted* such relationships but also that they wanted Lot to hand his guests over to them against his and his guests' will and against Jewish custom. They threatened violence; they pushed forward as if to break into the house; they were intent on sexual aggression, literally rape. If this passage is used against homosexuality, then it must in all fairness be against homosexual *rape,* and it could be used more appropriately against heterosexual rape than it could against *consenting* homosexual acts, the latter not being an issue in this story at all. We well know today that any kind of rape is not the result of a strong sex drive, although a sexual act is involved, but it is primarily the result of hostility and aggression and is almost exclusively a *male* act. It is a form of personal violence.

Yet even as bad as their requests and threatening acts were, it was apparently not the worst sin of the people in the city and not *the* reason God destroyed it. That decision had been made earlier (Gen. 18:16–20). Judging on the basis of later passages that look back upon the city at that time, the reasons were more widespread: "Behold, this was the guilt of . . . Sodom: she and her daughters had pride, surfeit of good, and prosperous ease, but did not aid the poor and needy. They were haughty, and did abominable things before me" (Ezek. 16:49–50). Although the writer of Ezekiel might well have had in mind the night of threatened sexual aggression when he spoke of "abominable things," he does not make any specific reference to homosexuality. He does come down hard on those who have much of the world's goods, who are proud of it, and who do not out of their abundance aid the poor and needy. Where does *that* leave many of *us* in the eyes of God? Just to emphasize the point, farther on in Ezekiel (chap.

22) is a listing of the sins of the people at the time of the writing of the book of Leviticus itself, among which are several sexual ones (22:10–12), but homosexuality is *not* among them.

Of the nine New Testament references to Sodom, not one mentions homosexuality specifically. Jude, verse 7, does say that the people of the city acted "immorally." The Greek word here refers to sexual immorality in general. The verse goes on to add that they "indulged in unnatural lust," literally "went after strange flesh," which might refer to homosexuality or, as some scholars suggest, to a desire to have sexual relations with angels ("strange flesh"), although, of course, they didn't seem to know that they were angels.[1] Second Peter 2:7 refers to the "licentiousness of the wicked," again the word translated "licentiousness" referring to sexual immorality in general. The other New Testament references to Sodom (Matt. 10:15 and its parallel, Luke 10:12; Matt. 11:23–24; Luke 17:29; Rom. 9:29; and Rev. 11:8) say nothing at all about homosexuality or any specific sin. They are all used as illustrations of the certainty of God's judgment on cities where people did not receive God's messengers.

Finally, those who read the King James version may see several places where the word "sodomite" is used. In every instance, according to Furnish, "the reference is to male prostitutes associated with places of worship," and therefore neither to homosexuality as a condition nor to homosexual relationships in the usual sense. The attacks against the male *and female* temple prostitutes in the Old Testament are not so much on the basis that they engaged in sexual acts, although that could be included, but that the acts reflected their worship of other gods.[2]

The point of all this is that the story of Sodom is a very poor example, indeed quite an inappropriate one, to cite as a condemnation of homosexuality as a condition (it says absolutely nothing about that) or of homosexual acts between consenting persons (it says nothing about that, either). It *can* be used to oppose homosexual desire that is linked to aggression. And, of course, if we are to use the Ezekiel verses, the entire story of Sodom can very well be used to condemn complacent luxury and neglect of the poor and needy, which is a frequent and persistent theme throughout the *entire* Old and *New* testaments, with literally scores of references, in stark contrast with the Bible's *very* infrequent statements about homosexual acts.

At this point, then, we have discovered only four references to homosexual acts in the entire Old Testament: the two in the

Leviticus passage (literally male with male, with the death penalty required, and with the whole Holiness Code now awaiting our examination of the New Testament in order to determine what is and is not valid for us today), the story in Judges (also involving violence), and the story of Sodom, with its horrible scene in which men seek to force sex on two angels disguised as men, by violence if necessary. It seems quite fair to say that the Old Testament has very little discussion of homosexual acts except as these may reflect the *worship of alien gods* or when they occur in the *context of aggression.* It is obvious that adultery is seen as far more destructive to family and larger social life, since both the act of adultery and coveting a neighbor's wife (are women then free to covet their neighbor's husband?) are condemned in the Ten Commandments but homosexual acts are not.

Moving to the New Testament, we are once again struck by the fact that it is rather difficult to find any statements there on homosexuality. *Jesus never mentions it at all.* He was hardly one to let serious sin go by unnoticed and unmentioned. Of course, Jesus didn't waste time cataloging sins and giving complete lists of them to a scribe to write down. He responded to specific situations that confronted him. We conclude, therefore, that either homosexuality was never an issue to him or, if it came up, the early church didn't think it was important enough to include in their record of what was essential to remember about Jesus regarding their church life and faith.

Besides the brief reference to Sodom in Jude, where, as I noted earlier, it might have referred to homosexual lust, only three other passages (in 1 Corinthians, 1 Timothy, and Romans) in the entire New Testament touch on the subject. In my comments on these, I am following for the most part Furnish's findings because his conclusions seem to be soundly based on the original language in its larger cultural and biblical context.

Furnish prefaces his discussion of these passages with some details about homosexual practices in the first-century Mediterranean world to arrive at and document three essential points that make up a rather common understanding of the meaning of homosexual acts then.[3]

> First, not only the terms, but also the concepts "homosexual" and "homosexuality" were unknown in Paul's day. These terms, like the terms "heterosexual," "heterosexuality," "bisexual," and "bisexuality," presume

an understanding of sexuality that was possible only with the advent of modern psychological and sociological analysis. The ancient writers . . . were operating without the vaguest conception of what we have learned to call "sexual orientation."[4]

In fact, the word *homosexuality* was not used until 1869 in an article written in German and was first used in English, according to some, twenty years later, or according to the *Oxford English Dictionary*, in 1892.

The distinction that we make today between a person's psychological and/or physiological *condition* of being and the acts that a person performs simply was not a possibility in the thought processes of the people of biblical times.

Therefore, Furnish's second point—merely an elaboration of the first—is that a homosexual act was understood then to be a perverse extension of heterosexual desire, the kind that occurs when heterosexual lust is so great that it is not adequately fulfilled by someone of the other sex. It was viewed as an act that reflected a person's excessive lust, lack of willpower, and, of course, for Jews and Christians, ungodliness.

Furnish's third point is that the first-century non-Christians who wrote about homosexual behavior saw it as necessarily involving either temple prostitution or one person's exploitation of another: subjects by rulers, slaves by masters, young boys by older men. Homosexual acts were understood as robbing the submissive partner of his maleness (remember, everything was written *by* males primarily *to* males) and was therefore literally still an exploitation, a robbing.

Given this social context and way of viewing behavior, it is not difficult to see that such practices would fall short of the standard of obedience and service to the God whose compassion and valuing of persons were made concrete and clear in Jesus. Christians would not be driven by lust, would not exploit others, would not rob them of vital aspects of their personhood.

To view the *condition* of homosexuality as an exclusive or primary sexual orientation established relatively early in life by whatever means and leading to a relationship of love, respect, intimacy, and commitment with someone else of similar *condition* was not part of first-century concepts or thinking or experience at all. Let's look now at the three specific texts.

First Corinthians 6:9, while clear to some, is not clear to others.

A comparison of just a half dozen of the different versions of the Bible shows the difficulty that even scholars have trying to determine the English words that most accurately convey Paul's intent when he wrote in Greek. Even though the Revised Standard Version, *The Jerusalem Bible*, and *The New English Bible*, to mention a few, all use words like "homosexuals" or "homosexual perverts" (both inaccurate translations), the original Greek has two distinct words for this concept. The first word, *malakos*, means "soft" or "weak," which prompted the King James version's use of the word "effeminate." (You can see the translators' stereotype of women in this word.) The use of this Greek word in nonbiblical writings of the times suggests that it was frequently used to refer to the passive partner in a male homosexual relationship.

Scroggs's detailed study of Greek writings over several centuries and his investigation of different types of sexual practices between older males and boys (pederasty) revealed that the word *malakoi*, "soft" or "effeminate," was used specifically to describe effeminate call boys, very young male prostitutes for older male clients, youth who had given up their male appearance and roles, "allowing themselves to be used as women."[5]

The second word, *arsenokoites*, means something like "males who go to bed," and when used in combination with the first word can refer to the sexual partner who assumes the traditional active role. Furnish's own translation reads, "... effeminate males, or men who have sex with them."[6] This, of course, indicates that the statement does have to do with male homosexual acts, and according to Scroggs, means the mature males who were the older clients of the "call boys."[7] These words were directed toward what was a Greek practice, absolutely abhorrent to Jews and later to the early church. This letter of Paul, of course, was addressed to a specific Greek congregation, many of whom were formerly worshipers of other gods.

These two words referring to a form of pederasty are found in a list that is representative (although not complete) of the behaviors of people who belong to this world, who are ungodly, who have not been "set apart for God's service, affirmed as righteous," and who "will not get into God's kingdom" (Furnish's translation).

When we realize the meaning that sexual acts between males had for people of Paul's time (filled with insatiable lust, exploitative, often engaging in temple prostitution, which indicates the worship of other gods, at times taking advantage of those with less social or personal power), it is clear that these acts cannot describe someone who is responding to God's loving call to enter into the kingdom. It is important to look at *other* examples of unrighteousness in this same list of those who will not enter the kingdom: idolaters, adulterers, drunkards, money-grabbers ("the greedy," RSV), and slanderers. *There is no indication that one of these examples of unrighteousness is more or less serious than another.* They simply illustrate behaviors that describe someone who *is not* eligible to enter the kingdom.

The list in 1 Timothy 1:9–10 is similar in intent, that is, to suggest a variety of behaviors, not to be an exhaustive cataloging of persons who, in the context in this letter, are those for whom God's law is designed, the "lawless and disobedient." One of the words used in this passage is the second of the two Greek words referred to in 1 Corinthians 6:9, "men who [actively] have sex with other men." Scroggs makes a case for the word's meaning here, a man who is a customer of a youth in a brothel. Also included in the 1 Timothy list are the "profane, . . . liars, perjurers."

These two lists (in 1 Corinthians and 1 Timothy) state *some* of the behaviors that are displeasing to God and that are symptomatic of sin. Homosexual behavior *as it was understood at that time* was displeasing to God.

The most frequently cited passage in the New Testament that condemns homosexual acts is Romans 1:26–27. It also has the one and only scriptural reference to homosexual relations between females. This section as a whole (Rom. 1:18–3:20) has a theological purpose, that is, to proclaim that we are all in need of the grace of God. Paul proceeds by first showing in 1:18–32 the wickedness of the Gentiles, and he does so in terms that are characteristic of a number of Jewish critics of the Gentile world at that time. The theme is that because they have not recognized God as their creator through the "natural" means around them (nature and the general moral order), they have been "given up by God" to all kinds of wickedness, that is, allowed by God to suffer the consequences of their behavior. The base *sin* is neither "homosexuality" nor any of the other behaviors listed; rather, it is failing to worship the true and living God. The results of not worshiping God are these kinds of behaviors, all of which are seen as conscious and willful. In other words, because they do not recognize the God that Christians now know in Christ, God has abandoned them to their various lusts, one of which is sexual. To engage in sexual relations with persons of the same sex is also one of these lusts, and again, it is a conscious decision to act out one's unrestrained passion in this way rather than heterosexually within marriage. If we assume that this is what homosexuality is, and *all* that it is, then this condition could be seen as in conflict with the behavior of one who does worship the living God.

To complete Paul's point, after he has described the Gentiles in this way, he hits the Jews: "*You* are no better. *All* have sinned. *None* can be justified on the basis of good works. We all can live *only* through the gracious forgiving acceptance of God as God is known through Jesus the Christ."

A summary of the logic of the New Testament position seems to be that if one denies the one God who is the creator and redeemer, one is then vulnerable to being dominated by one's own lusts and passions, one's own persistent self-seeking. So far, so good. But insatiable sexual lust, as Paul and his contemporaries believed, leads on beyond heterosexual activity to the choice of someone of one's own sex as a partner in a way that inevitably involves exploitation. The best scientific investigations today do not uphold this view of the nature of the *homosexual person* (chapter 8), nor is this view descriptive of all homosexual acts, although obviously they *may* be lustful and exploitative, just as heterosexual expressions sometimes are.

Now, what is the meaning for *us* in the two statements from Leviticus that were left hanging? It would seem that they and the New Testament, with Paul's addition of female homosexual acts but without the commandment concerning the death penalty, are not saying anything at all about the contemporary understanding of homosexual relationships: not temple prostitution, not pederasty. If we fit all the biblical references together, a summary of the scriptural position on homosexuality would seem to be that the Bible has *no explicit position at all* on homosexuality as a condition. It is something they knew nothing about and therefore could not have commented on. It is, however, a condition that we today know exists. Like other conditions and many modern situations about which the Bible has nothing to say, we are left with the necessity of seeking God's will in ways different from that of finding specific biblical statements of approval or disapproval. Where homosexual *acts* today are reflective of a disregard for the worship of God, where they are motivated only by the desire to fulfill one's own passion and are therefore selfish, where they are coercive and exploitive, then these fit the biblical descriptions of acts that are displeasing to God.

When persons are homosexual, however, this being a condition of persistent sexual orientation, possibly genetic influences, and certainly established early in life and developed over a long period of time, and when two homosexual persons are in love with each other, when they respect and appreciate each other, commit themselves to the well-being of each other, and desire sexual relationships with each other, we are left with a situation untouched by the biblical descriptions and injunctions. These persons, who may also desire to serve God, must seek God's will for themselves on the basis of the impact of the total message of the gospel as it is found in scripture, through prayer, and if possible, through discussion with other persons of faith.

I have pointed out that there are few references to homosexual acts in the Bible. These acts were understood in the very limited ways I have already explained. They were understood as lustful, exploitive acts involving the rejection of God. Therefore, they are not applicable to the *condition* of homosexuality as we know it today. Yet to say this is not the same as declaring that the Bible says homosexuality is okay. It does *not* explicitly state that. The emphasis of the scripture *as written* is on the side of God's plan for human beings involving heterosexual attraction and leading to a permanent marriage in which there is sexual fidelity. This seems to be the scripture's portrayal of the primary will of God. It is what is expected. The exceptions to this in the scripture are when a person in response to God's call to a particular mission in the world does not marry as a part of his or her effective carrying out of that mission (as with Jesus, Paul, and others). However, when the condition or situation is such that the will of God understood in this way is not possible for a person, and there are many such dilemmas in human life, the person of faith is not released from the obligation to seek what is *now* God's will for himself or herself from this time forward in the new situation or in a situation newly understood. Many homosexual persons today seem caught in this situation. Their *being* homosexual does not call for condemnation. The Bible *does not* condemn their condition. If they are serious about being Christian, they seek God's will for themselves, given the realities of their condition, and this must be between them and God.

It seems valid to apply the same biblical standards of *sexual behavior* to gays and lesbians that are applied to heterosexual persons.

The Bible is clear that promiscuity is a misuse of God's gift of sex and thus not a behavior that is consistent with being a part of God's people. The Bible is clear that we honor God through our faithful relationships with one another, including our sexual expression.

We need to recognize that many lesbians and gays are committed Christians and faithful members of the church. In response to this, I've heard many heterosexual Christians say, "But if they *really* are Christians, they would repent of their sin and change, because the Bible says———." Often the "change" those who feel this way have in mind is a change from homosexual orientation to a heterosexual one. They don't usually say it just like that. Rather, it's, "If they truly repent, then they won't be like *that* any longer; they won't keep 'doing it' [having sex] that way." The logic of those making these statements seems to be that because they don't change, they continue in sin, and thus they can't really be serious about being a Christian. What a trap! What if they *can't* change? Are they then forever barred from being Christian, a part of the people of God? Is there no way they can do God's will and maintain their sexual identity?

It seems to me that a somewhat comparable situation that is much closer to home to more Christians than those who are lesbian and gay is the status of those Christians who divorce and then remarry. Jesus is very clear (Matt. 19:9; Mark 10:11–12); "Whoever divorces . . . and marries another commits adultery." There seems to be no way to "interpret ourselves out" of that one. Now how does the person who wants to be a Christian respond? He or she repents of the sin and asks forgiveness. But wait. The persons *continue* to live in sin, do they not? What about solving the problem by divorcing this spouse? That doesn't seem to be in accord with God's will, either. This seems to be a trap, doesn't it?

But whoever we are—gay, lesbian, divorced, or remarried—others in whatever condition or situation we may be are not exempt from seeking God's will, now and *from this time forward*, and God's gracious invitations to us never cease. We are God's people.

Another approach to understanding the few verses of scripture that explicitly refer to homosexual acts is suggested by Frederick Gaiser. He offers Isaiah 56:1–8 as an example of an important method of interpretation, "Scripture interpreting Scripture," going beyond earlier law (Lev. 21:16–21, Deut. 23:1) to proclaim a new prophetic word: "the welcome to the foreigners and eunuchs in Isaiah 56 (verses 5–7) apparently overturning both tradition and the Torah."[8]

To those who were formerly denied admission to the worshiping people of God the prophet declares a new word, an invitation based on God's grace and not because we are without "blemish" (the reason that many could not approach to make an offering to God [Leviticus 21]), to become a part of God's people if they are faithful to the covenant. Such participation in the life of the people of God is not any person's or group's *right;* rather it is the result of God's desire to gather "all peoples" (Isa. 56:7) and the people's desire to accept the invitation and willingness to accept the terms.

Gaiser reminds us that Jesus also transformed the Law, or even transcended it (Matt. 5:21–22, 28–29, 31–32). People enter the kingdom of God in response to the Spirit, not because of their legal obedience (p. 288). Gaiser understands gays and lesbians to be comparable to the foreigners and eunuchs, thus among "*all* peoples" whom God would gather together as God's own. They enter the kingdom when they "hold fast to the Covenant," which, among other things, means accepting the New Testament standard of sexual behavior: "committed, loving, and just" relationships, comparable in every way to the ideal stated for heterosexual marriage.[9]

I believe it is essential for parents to distinguish between their own *personal* negative feelings toward the homosexuality of their son or daughter (lack of understanding, the loss of the future they had taken for granted, revulsion, anger, disapproval, even condemnation) and what the Bible actually does and does not say about homosexual acts. I do not believe that the Bible, carefully and prayerfully read, is the source of the reaction of panic and dread and attack on homosexual persons. These strong negative reactions are parents' (and others') own personal ones, for their own personal reasons: the breakdown of their perception of reality concerning their son or daughter, their fear of what this means for the way they have lived their lives as parents, the changing of their expected future, their fear of social disapproval.

The impact of this chapter dealing with the Bible is that a harsh condemnation of homosexuality (or even any condemnation) is not supported by any passage in the Bible, nor does the scripture place any particular focus on it as one of the "major sins." My intent, however, is not to try to convince parents that the Bible *approves* either of the homosexual condition (since it doesn't mention it) or of homosexual acts (since the *acts as they* understood them *are* condemned). Reasonable and sincere Christian people may still, on the basis of the Bible as they understand it, or on what they might refer to as the "natural order of things," or for certain other reasons see homosexuality as opposed to God's primary will, a condition that was not intended in creation. But as loving Christians and parents and family members, they should know that love (reread 1 Corinthians 13) requires an attempt to understand homosexual persons and certainly entails caring for them as we would any other person who is our "neighbor," for they are those whom God loves. The Bible requires this.

In the midst of the Bible's quite rare disapproval of certain kinds of homosexual acts (and many kinds of heterosexual acts), its silence about homosexuality as a condition and about loving and committed homosexual relationships, a strong voice still comes through loud and clear: "Judge not, that you be not judged. For with the judgment you pronounce you will be judged" (Matt. 7:1–2). Or perhaps even more apt is the conclusion of Paul's listing of many of the possible symptoms arising out of the condition of those who have forsaken the worship of the living God (Rom. 1:18–32). Romans 2:1 goes on: "Therefore you have no excuse, whoever you are, when you judge another; for in passing judgment upon the other you condemn yourself . . . ."

But even behind that warning is the compassionate God who was the source of the life of Jesus and the source of our own life and the lives of our children. When God's love for us and our children is known, then the power for change in our attitudes and feelings and the power for reconciliation within our families begins to be felt: "Beloved, let us love one another; for love is of God, and the one who loves is born of God and knows God. . . . We love, because God first loved us" (1 John 4:7, 19).

10 *What Does Our Child Want of Us?*

I was sitting at a table having a lively and serious conversation with two gay men, one in his late twenties, the other in his thirties. They were interested in sharing with me the significant details, past and present, of their lives. The younger had been describing the separation from his parents that he had felt early in his life. Well he might! He had been sent to a private school a great distance from his home at a very young age. He saw his parents only once or twice a year. But the distance was emotional as well as physical. As he grew older, along with his increasing recognition that he was gay, he became aware of the resentment he felt toward his parents. His father was highly authoritarian, and they had great difficulty talking. After this young man became an adult and had settled completely into his gay life, with a great deal of fear he told his parents about his sexual orientation.

I interrupted to ask the question that I, of course, was extremely interested in: "What was the reason you told them? After all, you've told me about their sending you away for most of your childhood and teenage years, your resentment about this, some of the other ways they treated you. Were you interested in developing a better relationship with them?" The young man looked very surprised at this question, and the tone of his voice seemed to suggest that such a question was entirely unnecessary: "Of course!" Of course, nearly all children, of whatever age, long for a good relationship with their parents if they don't have it already. Regardless of what has or has not gone on between them, it is impossible for children—whether they are four, fourteen, twenty-four, or forty-four—to escape the reality that they are children of their own parents, emotionally bound and emotionally reactive to them. Of course, under some circumstances, teenage and adult children may need to put distance between themselves and their parents, get away physically, or change the nature of the emotional ties. In fact, it is inevitable that the nature of the emotional ties will change. It is also true, to be sure, that there will be occasions when the relationship is so frustrating, so angering over a long period of time that a young man or woman will finally give up. "I don't care what my parents think or how they feel anymore. I've had it!" This unfortunately can and does occasionally happen. But nearly always there remains a yearning on both sides for a relationship of mutual honesty, respect, friendship, and ease of being together that allows a person to be himself or herself and be loved and accepted, a full and genuine member of the family.

"Of course!" The desire to develop a better relationship continues even, or perhaps especially, when there's been estrangement. Often a deepening separation occurs when the young person is gay or lesbian. Sometimes the separation is obvious—marked by constant anger and conflict, arguments, unpleasantness, or cool distance. I have seen many instances of these responses. But very often it's not that way at all. Rather, those involved feel a gradually growing sense of discomfort. If the son or daughter has already left home, is at college, or is working, the visits home begin to grow shorter or decrease in an effort to protect both the parents and oneself. Being with their parents and continuing to pretend or at least allowing them to continue to think that their son or daughter is someone he or she is not; telling about friends, but being very careful not to tell too much about certain ones; about activities, but in a guarded way; about one's roommate, but—this feels like very dangerous ground. All this caution, guardedness, defensiveness, and occasional lying leads to a great deal of anxiety and tension. It is difficult to have good, free-flowing conversations. It takes the fun out of the visit. It stands in the way of the developing adult-to-adult relationship that can be so satisfying for parents and their mature children.

The son or daughter also discourages visits from the parents. What would the son or daughter do to entertain the parents? Invite friends over? Go out to a favorite bar? Attend the Metropolitan Community Church on Sunday morning? And if one is living with a lover, what does one do? Send the lover away? Spend several days trying to pretend that they're "just friends"? It is tense, awkward, artificial. It is a lie, and that creates a feeling of guilt.

If there is a particular lover in the picture, if there is a developing and committed relationship, it is only natural that they want to do more and more things together, just as young people want to do in a heterosexual relationship. It is natural to want to take a loved person home, introduce the person to one's parents, share the meaningful relationship with them. This is especially true when holidays arrive that have traditionally been family affairs: Thanksgiving, Christmas, one's own or a parent's birthday.

A man in his late thirties, a college teacher, formerly married and a father, came out a few years ago. In a talk he gave to a group of college counselors and administrators he said, "The most difficult thing about being homosexual is one's relationship to one's parents and other family members." Many young people who have been struggling with their own sexual identity over the years, who have been troubled by their strong feelings of attraction to persons of the same sex, who from time to time have had homosexual experiences, have felt very isolated and alienated from their own families, from their churches, from many of their lifelong friends, from society as a whole. They have had to struggle and work alone to try to make sense out of their own being. It has been agonizing and lonely, and they haven't always known whom they could trust. Deep within themselves they have realized that being loved, accepted, and supported by members of their own families, especially their parents, is central to their coming to terms with themselves, breaking down the walls of isolation, gaining a sense of well-being and a constructive direction for their lives. They are fearful for themselves and their parents when they think about opening up this issue for discussion. They plan for it but then don't initiate the conversation. This is repeated many times. They rehearse the words and imagine the reactions. Those reactions range from the best ("You're our child and we love you. You can always be yourself with us.") to the worst (weeping, denunciation, banishment). In their minds they alternately imagine what they desire so passionately and then their most dreaded predictions.

Some never get around to initiating such a conversation, leaving the parents to discover the truth in some other way or to live with unspoken suspicion or perhaps never to know. Some finally take the plunge, fear and all. According to a young friend who took an informal survey of her friends, only 11 percent had told their parents, 27 percent of the parents had found out in some other way, and 61 percent of the parents had neither been told nor found out in any other way. Since that informal survey was carried out many years ago, I believe that a higher percentage are now telling their parents and telling them earlier, though not more easily.

When I have talked with homosexual persons about their desires, with rare exceptions they indicate a wish to be able to talk about their sexual orientation openly with their parents and know that they will still be loved and accepted as their parents' child and a genuine member of the family in every respect. Their great conflict concerns whether they can have a better relationship by telling or by not telling. Either route is extremely difficult and each has its particular tensions. But the desire to have a good relationship with their parents and other family members is nearly universal, even though a few have come to believe that such a goal is unattainable and they have given up.

What do these teenagers, these young adults, and sometimes older adults really want? They want some different things, of course. Some might want their parents to direct them to a helpful professional or to someone who can help them figure themselves out. They want to know for sure whether or not they are lesbian or gay. Some are not sure, or they may even think they are headed that way but genuinely want to see whether they can become heterosexual. Some will definitely be gay and will *not* want to change their sexual orientation. But even so, they would like help in understanding themselves. Some who are promiscuous are thoroughly disgusted with the way they relate sexually and, while remaining gay, would like to learn how to give up their present style of making random sexual contacts and begin to establish long-lasting, meaningful relationships with a sexual partner.

But numerous homosexual persons do not feel in need of the type of help I've been describing. With both groups, however, there is usually a common desire to have the type of relationship with their parents that a child of any age would want to have, and in so many instances, this calls for reconciliation. As Christians, "God, . . . through Christ reconciled us to himself *and gave us the ministry of reconciliation*" (2 Cor. 5:18).

They would like, first of all, to feel that they can be honest with their parents, including, but not limited to, being honest about their own homosexuality. Such honesty presupposes that regardless of what parents hear from their sons or daughters, they will first attempt to understand what their children's experiences are like to them. Assuming that most parents will experience many of the thoughts and feelings I have described in earlier chapters, these feelings need not stand in the way of that attempt to understand. That attempt is the first step in maintaining any good relationship, as well as being the first step in reconciliation—the attempt to *understand* the other. The lesbian or gay child likewise has a similar responsibility to understand the parents.

Second, the gay or lesbian son or daughter wants to be accepted for who he or she is. Not many teenagers and adults are so unrealistic as to expect that their parents will *approve* of their behavior. After all, they don't approve of some of their parents' behavior either, nor do they even approve of all their own. But not any one of us, as human beings, wants to be judged as a person wholly on the basis of only one aspect of our lives. Time and time again, I have heard homosexual persons say something like, "I want them to look at me as who I am totally, not just at my sexual preference. After all, I'm the same person now that I was before they knew about this."

Our sons or daughters, whether homosexual *or* heterosexual, may be doing things in ways quite different from our ways, may be doing things that we truly believe are wrong, may not be fulfilling their potential. They may even be in serious trouble, and this pains and sometimes angers us. But even if we don't understand or approve of the fact that our son or daughter is lesbian or gay, he or she may also in other respects be living a very responsible life, have high moral standards, be loving and sensitive, and have a deep and meaningful Christian faith. Even if we are deeply distressed by their *homosexuality*, they want us to see them as the *whole* persons they are.

Third, I reiterate that they want to be as much members of the family in their own parents' eyes as anyone else is, as much as the child who meets all your expectations, as much as their brothers and sisters who have married and had children.

Parents usually find themselves in the midst of a crisis in the literal sense of the word when they discover that a son or daughter is lesbian or gay. Their self-images, their images of the family, their reputation, the family system as a system—all are threatened. One way of attempting to deal with a crisis is to deny the reality of what has taken place and to behave, relate, and communicate rigidly in the ways they have done before. This strategy can work to the detriment of the total family. Spontaneous loving relationships are transformed into anxious and strained pretense. This is not at all to say that the people cease to love. However, the openness and warmth is covered and bound by strained behavior, and beneath it all is great pain and a longing for reconciliation.

Another way of dealing with a crisis requires our feeling the pain and allowing it to be the stimulus that forces us to reexamine ourselves as individuals and as a family system, allowing the crisis to crack us open to be the *human* selves that we are, vulnerable to one another, yet trusting one another's responses. The crisis has the potential of pushing us to a level of informational exchange, awareness of our feelings, and the communication of our feelings that perhaps we have never had before and that would lead us into a new quality of loving relationship with one another. This is something else that your homosexual son or daughter probably wants of you and of themselves in relationship to you.

The crises precipitated by the discovery that your son or daughter is homosexual may provide you and your family, in the midst of your disappointment and anger and confusion and pain and sadness, the opportunity for constructive change. The Bible does not offer protection from a painful or even a dangerous crisis to those who respond to God's love for them. It does promise that nothing "will be able to separate us from the love of God in Christ Jesus our Lord," and it affirms that "we know that in everything God works for good with those who love him" (Rom. 8:39, 28).

The discovery that your son or daughter is homosexual may actually be a crisis of faith itself. The inevitable question of Why? arises spontaneously in the minds and on the lips of many. "Why me, Lord? Why that person? Why us? Why are you punishing us this way? How could you be all-loving and all-powerful and let something like this happen?" Natural cries of anger and anguish like these may lead to anger at God, denial of God, unrelieved guilt even after many prayers for forgiveness, a lessening of the meaning of participation in the community of faith, the church, even withdrawal from the church. It is possible for us to give ourselves over to these feelings and our faith diminishes, becomes less meaningful, and our whole life becomes limited in ways it was not limited before. Unfortunately, some people allow themselves to continue to live at this level. However, such a crisis, with its attendant feelings and questions, can drive persons to reexamine the basics of faith, to do a more studied reading and discus-

sion of the Bible, and to take an honest look at themselves in relationship to God in light of what they are now in the process of discovering.

In reading the Bible, you have the possibility of sharing somewhat my own conclusion—the one elaborated upon in chapter 9.
While this view of the Bible's dealing with the issue of homosexuality may not change your immediate personal feelings, I hope
that it might provide the perspective that can facilitate your grappling with your feelings and working lovingly and constructively
within your partly old, partly new relationship with your child.

On the other hand, like many other conscientious people, as a
result of your inevitable conditioning by society, as a result of
your best understanding of the scripture, which brings you to a
position different from mine, or from reasoning on the basis of
what you understand to be natural or God's design in creation,
you may never reach a point where you can approve of any homosexual acts. You may genuinely believe them to be morally
wrong. But you can learn to live well with your daughter or son,
just as we all do with ourselves and other family and friends every
day, none of us being perfect in the sense of being just exactly as
we'd like ourselves and others to be.

If this is where you are, and if this is where you come out even
after a prolonged process of study and discussion, then you are
faced with the task of reconciling your beliefs with the relationship that you truly want to have with your own son or daughter.
Few people are willing to give up a relationship with their children in the name of faith, although I have been involved with at
least one family in which this seemed to be the case. It was a
tragedy: genuinely good people, Christian people, with deep love
for their son, but feeling deeply that he was so wrong that they
could no longer welcome him home. Extremely sad.

Your difficult task is to make a clear distinction between that
behavior you believe to be morally wrong, or sin, and your son or
daughter, who from your point of view, is a sinner, *but who still is
your child.* Regardless of the choices of our own children, and they
will make them about their own lives, we also want to experience
the two-way communication of love in our relationships with
them. In fact, I believe that faith itself includes within it the imperative to move toward developing a loving relationship between parent and child.

Therefore, no matter what your sincere belief is about what the

Bible says concerning homosexuality and regardless of whether you believe it to be a sin or not, I believe that your awareness of the whole thrust of the biblical message and your continuing attempt to understand what it is saying to you in your situation at this time will lead you to understand that God *is,* God is *love,* God's love is *powerful,* and that God never stops seeking us or working with us to bring about our reconciliation with God and with one another. God is the one who offers to us all in whatever circumstances a new tomorrow.

In the midst of your present experience, whatever questions, thoughts, and feelings you might have, however the relationships in your family might be at this moment, it is possible to share the faith of the apostle Paul: "We are afflicted in every way, but not crushed; perplexed, but not driven to despair; persecuted, but not forsaken; struck down, but not destroyed. . . . For while we live we are always being given up to death for Jesus' sake, so that the life of Jesus may be manifested in our mortal flesh. . . . So we do not lose heart" (2 Cor. 4:8–9, 11, 16).

Many parents have allowed their genuine love for and commitment to their son or daughter to sustain them in the demanding process of working through all that reconciliation entails. It is often a long process, lasting from many months to a few years. It involves allowing themselves to feel and express their strong and conflicting emotions. It means negotiating and renegotiating the tensions within the family. It means numerous discussions and, often enough, even arguments with the lesbian or gay young person or adult. It means having to bear periods of emotional and sometimes physical distancing. The successful resolution of the process necessitates getting through to the other side on the numerous occasions you may well want to give up. This process may also include the questioning of God, uneasiness with members of the church congregation, and feeling a loss of faith. But the love and commitment to the son or daughter will prevail, and faith will still operate to guide and sustain you even in periods when only its absence is felt.

In the final analysis, parents must "not lose heart." Their reward will be the quality of relationship with their son or daughter that all parents and all children of whatever age long for: mutual love and respect and friendship and a sense of belonging. Numerous parents and their homosexual sons and daughters have reported such reconciliation. It is worth working toward.

"Beloved, I am writing you no new commandment, but an old commandment which you had from the beginning. . . . And this commandment we have from him, that whoever loves God should love his brother [sister, son, daughter, neighbor] also" (1 John 2:7; 4:21).

Notes

Chapter 1. Oh, No!

1. Elisabeth Kübler-Ross, *On Death and Dying* (New York: Macmillan, 1969), 34.
2. C. Murray Parkes, "The First Year of Bereavement," *Psychiatry* 33 (1970): 448.

Chapter 2. We've Lost Our Child

1. Charles A. Silverstein, *A Family Matter: A Parent's Guide to Homosexuality* (New York: McGraw-Hill, 1977), 32–33.
2. These stages are based on the research of C. Murray Parkes, "The First Year of Bereavement," *Psychiatry* 33 (1970): 448.

Chapter 3. Is Our Child Really Gay?

1. *Homosexuality* (New York: Sex Information and Education Council of the U.S., n.d.).
2. *Changing Views of Homosexuality*, no. 563 (New York: Public Affairs Committee, n.d.).
3. Emphasis added; B.R.S. Rosser, "A Scientific Understanding of Sexual Orientation with Implications for Pastoral Ministry," *Word and World* (summer 1994): 246–57.
4. William R. Stanton, *Human Sexuality: An Encyclopedia* (New York: Garland Publishing, 1994), 64.
5. Wayne Dynes, *Encyclopedia of Homosexuality* (New York: Garland Publishing, 1990), 146.

Chapter 7. What Will People Think?

1. Alan P. Bell and Martin S. Weinberg, *Homosexualities* (New York: Simon & Schuster, 1978), 63–64, 66–67.

Chapter 8. What Causes Homosexuality Anyway?

1. Irving Bieber et al., *Homosexuality: A Psychoanalytic Study* (New York: Basic Books, 1962), 162.

Chapter 9. But Doesn't the Bible Condemn It?

1. Victor P. Furnish, "The Bible and Homosexuality," in *Homosexuality in the Church,* edited by Jeffrey S. Siker (Louisville: Westminster John Knox Press, 1994), 20.
2. Victor P. Furnish, *The Moral Teaching of Paul* (Nashville: Abingdon, 1979), 57.
3. For even greater detail, see Robin Scroggs, *The New Testament and Homosexuality: Contextual Background for Contemporary Debate* (Philadelphia: Fortress Press, 1983).
4. Furnish, *Moral Teaching,* 65.
5. Scroggs, *New Testament and Homosexuality,* 42.
6. Furnish, *Moral Teaching,* 69.
7. Scroggs, *New Testament and Homosexuality,* 108.
8. Frederick J. Gaiser, "A New Word on Homosexuality? Isaiah 56:1–8 as Case Study," *Word and World* (summer 1994): 282.
9. Gaiser, "A New Word?" 291–92.

Additional Resources

The following list includes some books written specifically for parents and family members and some that are written for church members in general. It is a very brief and selective list. I have deliberately omitted many excellent longer and more technical books. A much greater number of those are available now than in 1980. In addition, I must apologize to a number of authors for not including their books—books that might appropriately be listed here but were not simply because I was not aware of them. Attempting to become familiar with the entire literature of this field would have been an impossible task in the time allotted.

As you read two or three of the books on this list and begin to move through some of the emotional and relational stages that we have discussed in this book, I believe it would make sense for you to consider reading some of the longer and more technical books. I suggest that you consult the bibliographies in the books below or in other books mentioned in the text.

I also believe that most parents will find little value in reading books that describe in detail the "gay lifestyle." Thus none of those are recommended for your reading *at this time*.

Specifically for Parents

Fairchild, Betty, and Nancy Hayward. *Now That You Know: What Every Parent Should Know About Homosexuality*. San Diego: Harcourt Brace Jovanovich, 1986.

> A longer and more detailed book that is probably the very next book a parent should read. There is sound, although not undisputed, information about homosexuality as a condition, as well as

a chapter that looks at the relevant biblical passages and the positions of a number of churches on the issue of homosexuality. The book contains a great deal of case material, and it is easily read and very helpful.

Griffin, Carolyn Welch, with Marian J. and Arthur G. Wirth. *Beyond Acceptance*. Englewood Cliffs, N.J.: Prentice-Hall, 1986.

Personal statements of the authors concerning their own experiences, as well as references to other parents' experiences. They discuss their reactions to finding out that a child was gay or lesbian and tell what helped them most. They also discuss issues surrounding religion and the rest of the family. Clearly written.

Muller, Ann. *Parents Matter: Parents' Relationships with Lesbian Daughters and Gay Sons*. Tallahassee, Flor.: The Naiad Press, 1987.

An easily read book based on a survey of parents and their gay and lesbian children in the Chicago area. Although certain conclusions cannot be generalized from such a limited sample, the reported experiences of parent and children, given in their own words, are common ones and can be helpful to parents who have discovered only recently that their child is gay or lesbian.

Silverstein, Charles A. *A Family Matter: A Parent's Guide to Homosexuality*. New York: McGraw-Hill Book Co., 1977.

This book, written by a psychotherapist, was first recommended to me by several gay persons who found it an excellent description of themselves, their self-image, their struggles, their relationships with their parents. It is competently done and generally helpful. However, I *do not* recommend that this book be the first or second book you read. I believe that many parents will be hindered in their own process of resolving their conflicted feelings by one emotionally charged chapter. However, after some further reading and after work on yourself and between husband and wife and discussion with your teenage or adult child, I believe that there are important insights to be gained from Silverstein.

Homosexuality, the Bible, and the Church

Furnish, Victor Paul. *The Moral Teaching of Paul: Selected Issues*, revised. Nashville: Abingdon Press, 1985, chapter 3, "Homosexuality."

The best single brief piece of writing I have yet seen on a biblical view of homosexual acts. The position is presented in chapter 9 of this book, but Furnish's entire chapter is worth reading.

Scanzoni, Letha, and Virginia Ramey Mollenkott. *Is the Homosexual My Neighbor? Another Christian View*. New York: Harper & Row, 1978.

A must for the Christian. Written by committed Christian persons, this book discusses the variety of issues surrounding homosexual persons and homosexuality: the social setting, society's reactions, some of the knowledge we have about homosexuality, a chapter on the Bible, the response of churches, a "homosexual Christian ethic." Every book on this topic contains controversial material, and this one does also, but it is easily read, competently done, and is important. Has an excellent bibliography.

Siker, Jeffrey S., ed. *Homosexuality in the Church: Both Sides of the Debate.* Louisville, Ky.: Westminster John Knox Press, 1994.

Sections of the book discuss the Bible, church tradition, moral theology, scientific information, several official denominational statements, and other issues. Two chapters deal with the Bible: Richard B. Hays, "Awaiting the Redemption of Our Bodies: The Witness of Scripture Concerning Homosexuality," and Victor Paul Furnish, "The Bible and Homosexuality: Reading the Texts in Context." See also the two contrasting chapters on scientific information and its interpretation: Stanton L. Jones and Don E. Workman, "Homosexuality: The Behavioral Sciences and the Church," and Chandler Burr, "Homosexuality and Biology."

AIDS

Allen, Jimmy. *Burden of a Secret.* Nashville: Moorings, 1995.

By a well-known Southern Baptist minister, this book presents their family's painful struggle with the death from AIDS of a daughter-in-law and two grandchildren. The AIDS was initially contracted through a blood transfusion by the young mother during a pregnancy. There was the additional shock of discovering that one of her sons was gay and had AIDS. A moving story of the struggle of faith in the midst of their disruptions.

Schwarz, Ruth. *AIDS Medical Guide.* San Francisco AIDS Foundation, P.O. Box 426182, San Francisco, Calif. 94142–6182, 3d ed., 1992.

A very concise, clear 37-page book presenting an overview of all relevant medical information in language a layperson can understand. It also lists a number of useful resources. A physician who treats persons with AIDS might have several copies on hand and give you a copy. If you cannot locate a copy this way, order from the address above.

AIDS: A Guide for Survival. Harris County Medical Society/Houston Academy of Medicine, 1133 M.D. Anderson Blvd., Houston, Tex. 77030; (713) 790–1838.

A similar, somewhat older, but longer book (87 pages), including a glossary, bibliography, and a list of resources.

Support Groups

Parents, Family, and Friends of Lesbians and Gays (P-FLAG)

A nationwide organization of 360 or more local chapters in the United States, with a number in other countries. Support groups meet regularly; literature available. Look in your local telephone book or call the national office to find out where the group closest to you is located. National P-FLAG Office: 1012 14th Street N.W., Suite 700, Washington, D.C. 20005; (202) 638–4200.

Videotape

"After Goodbye—An AIDS Story." KERA-TV, Dallas, Tex., 1993.

A very moving production featuring beautiful music by the Turtle Creek Chorale of Dallas, approximately 100 voices of gays and lesbians, a large number of whom are HIV-positive or who have AIDS, and whose ranks continually need to be replenished because of the frequency of deaths. There are also several scenes and dialogues of a support group of parents whose children have AIDS or who have died of AIDS. You may order this video from KERA-TV, 3000 Harry Hines Blvd., Dallas, Tex. 75201. The cost is $24.95.

Also be sure to consult your local phone book under AIDS. If you live in a smaller community that lacks these resources, call the National AIDS Hotline: 1–800-342-AIDS.